B¹

This book has been made possible by
the generosity of Lord Vestey and
Mr Edmund Vestey.

SMITHFIELD
·PAST & PRESENT·
ALEC FORSHAW & THEO BERGSTRÖM

ROBERT HALE · LONDON

The right of Alec Forshaw to be identified as
author of this work has been asserted by him
in accordance with the Copyright, Designs and
Patents Act 1988.

Robert Hale Limited
Clerkenwell House
Clerkenwell Green
London EC1R 0HT

British Library Cataloguing in Publication Data

Forshaw, Alec, *1951–*
    Smithfield: past and present. – 2nd ed.
    1. London (City). Smithfield, to 1980
    I. Title   II. Bergström, Theo
    942.1′2

    ISBN 0-7090-4051-2

Printed in Great Britain by
St Edmundsbury Press Limited, Bury St Edmunds, Suffolk
Bound by WBC Bookbinders Limited

CONTENTS

6 *The Watch House in Giltspur Street at the turn of the century, with bluecoat boys eyeing the camera.* **G.L.C.**

ILLUSTRATIONS

INTRODUCTION

Most people will have heard of Smithfield; to the majority it conjures up the famous meat market. For many Londoners, it is probably where their local butcher or restaurateur buys his meat. However, a slice of meat on the plate reveals little about the character, origins or future of Smithfield, or about the other institutions and activities which rub shoulders with the market.

Right in the heart of modern London, Smithfield is a remarkably small and compact area. Surrounded by busy roads, it is surprisingly off the beaten track. Although it is becoming fashionable, not least for its new restaurants and unusual pubs, it is not a major tourist honeypot.

The meat market physically dominates the area. Yet within a stone's throw of the market, just on the other side of the square, lies St. Bartholomew's Hospital, London's oldest hospital on its original site; around the corner in Charterhouse Square is The Charterhouse, with its fascinating history and marvellous collection of ancient buildings; a short distance up St. John's Lane is the gateway to the former Priory of St. John, now the British headquarters of The Order of St. John of Jerusalem. Beside the market stands the magnificent priory church of St. Bartholomew-the-Great, London's oldest and most beautiful parish church, and nearby are the churches of St. Botolph's Aldersgate, St. Sepulchre's Newgate and St. Andrew's Holborn, as well as the Old Bailey and the headquarters of the Post Office. The commercial life of the area is richly diverse; printing, textiles, metal work, jewellery, watches and clocks, are all long established here, but fast declining; interspersed among these trades are numerous pubs, cafés, shops, agents and brokers serving the area and office-based newcomers.

Smithfield has an immense history and tradition, much of which is still strongly in evidence in the existing streets, buildings and activities. Having largely escaped the Great Fire of London and the devastation of the war-time blitz, it also avoided the worst of the building boom of the 1960s and 70s which assaulted so much of central London.

This second edition of *Smithfield Past and Present* comes ten years after its first publication, and includes a new chapter describing what has happened. For an area with a living history stretching back nearly two millennia – as a 'smooth field' on the edge of Roman Londinium – a decade may not seem long. To those close to the ground they have been ten years of great change. The next ten may bring yet more, threatening the fundamental character of Smithfield and its survival as an identifiable enclave of central London. As an amalgam of past and present the book encourages a greater appreciation of those buildings, activities and traditions which survive; the message remains the same but more urgent.

Alec Forshaw

10　*Smithfield meat market in 1895, looking from Hart's Corner along Charterhouse Street.*　**G.L.C.**

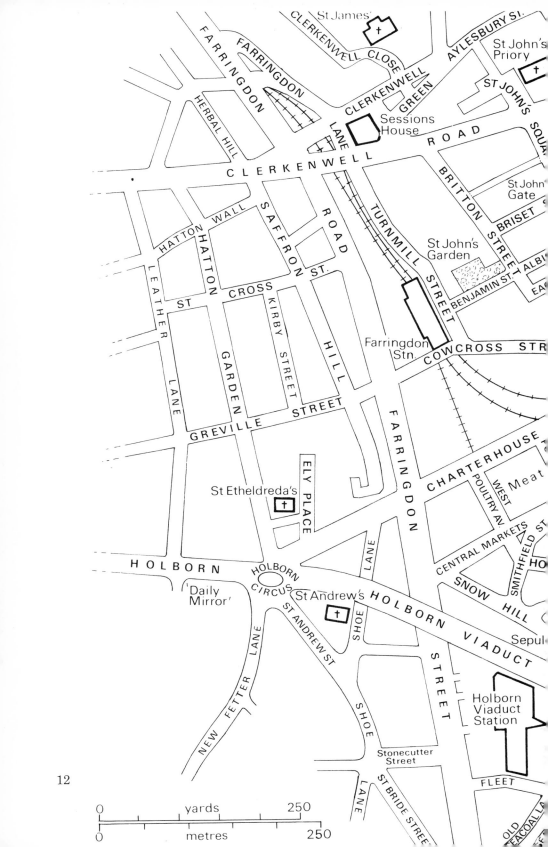

St James'
CLERKENWELL CLOSE
AYLESBURY ST.
St John's Priory
FARRINGDON
FARRINGDON
CLERKENWELL GREEN
ST JOHN'S SQUARE
HERBAL HILL
Sessions House
CLERKENWELL LANE
ROAD
St John Gate
ST JOHN'S ROAD
BRITTON STREET
BRISET
HATTON WALL
SAFFRON
ROAD
St John's Garden
St John Gate
LEATHER ST
HATTON
CROSS ST.
KIRBY STREET
HILL
TURNMILL STREET
BENJAMIN ST.
ALBI
EA
HATTON
GARDEN
Farringdon Stn.
COWCROSS STR
GREVILLE STREET
STREET
LANE
FARRINGDON
CHARTERHOUSE
WEST
POULTRY AV.
Meat
ELY PLACE
St Etheldreda's
CENTRAL MARKETS
SMITHFIELD ST.
HO
HOLBORN
LANE
HOLBORN CIRCUS
SNOW HILL
'Daily Mirror'
St Andrew's
HOLBORN VIADUCT
Sepul
NEW FETTER LANE
ST ANDREW ST
SHOE LANE
STREET
Holborn Viaduct Station
SHOE
Stonecutter Street
ST BRIDE STREET
FLEET
LANE
OLD
EACOALLA

12

0   yards   250
0   metres   250

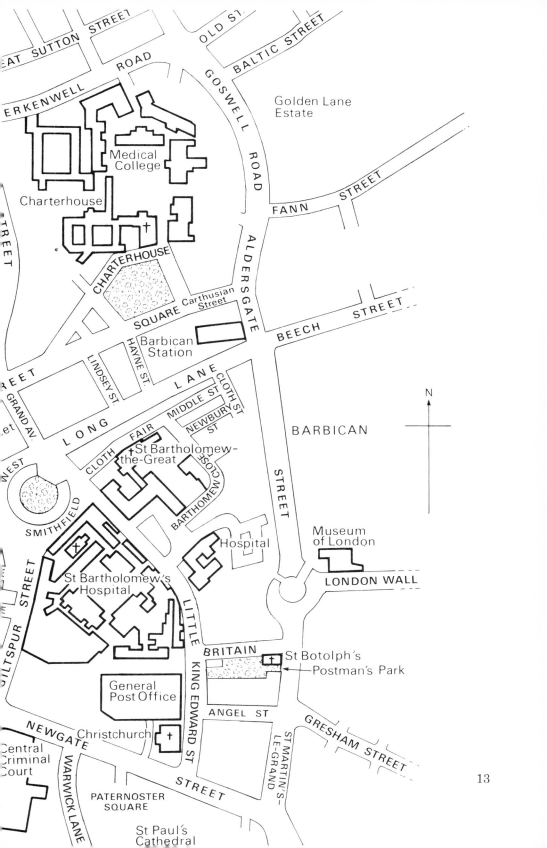

14 *St. Bartholomew's Gatehouse, built in 1559 after the demolition of the church nave – one of London's few surviving Tudor buildings.* **Theo Bergström**

CHAPTER·1· ORIGINS & DEVELOPMENT

THE ROMANS AND THE MIDDLE AGES

The story of Smithfield starts with the Romans. True enough, over one hundred pieces of Bronze Age pottery dating from 1500 B.C. were found recently during the archaeological dig on the Angel Street–Newgate Street site (now being developed by the Post Office), but as yet there is no evidence of any settlement to go with them.

In A.D. 43, the Romans built the first bridge across the Thames, almost on the site of the present London Bridge, and a fort to defend the crossing. This square garrison was roughly where the Barbican is today, just east of Smithfield. Roman roads ran north to St. Albans and Lincoln, east to Colchester, and west to Silchester.

Beyond the open ground we know today as Smithfield, the Fleet River, a tributary of the Thames, formed a useful, defendable barrier. From its source at a spring in Kenwood on Hampstead Heath, it flowed south to King's Cross and along the present line of Farringdon Road to join the Thames where Blackfriars Bridge is now. Two thousand years later the stream still flows as any walker on the heath will know, but its course to the Thames is buried in culverts and sewers.

With a bridge and a navigable river, London became a flourishing port and in A.D. 190 a wall was built to defend the expanding Londinium; it was finished by A.D. 220. The wall incorporated the early fort from where it ran south and west to the Fleet, and east to the Tower. It was built of stone and rubble, twenty feet high and eight feet thick, faced with Kentish ragstone brought by barge up the Medway and Thames.

A splendidly preserved stretch of the Roman wall survives below ground level in the Post Office yard next to St. Bartholomew's Hospital, and can be viewed by appointment. Construction of the recent

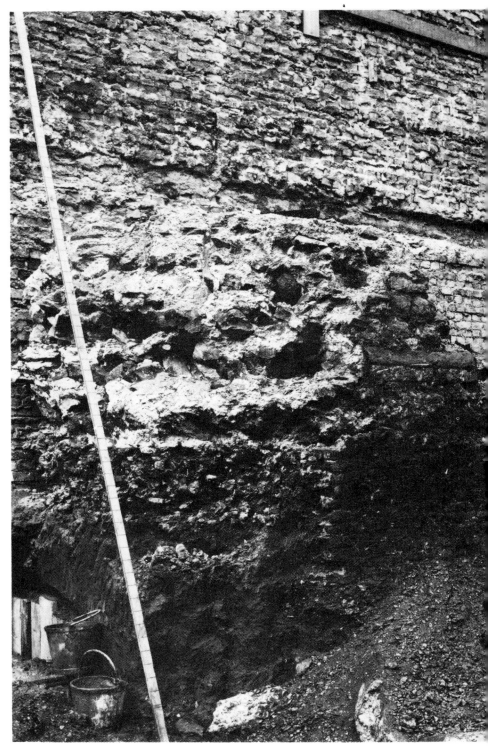

16   *Part of old London Wall, uncovered in
      1905 while digging foundations for
      the Post Office in King Edward Street:
      now preserved in the basement.* **G.L.C.**

extension to the Old Bailey also revealed fine Roman remains, a small part of which has been preserved in the east extension of the court.

Within the wall were six gates: Ludgate, Newgate, Aldersgate, Cripplegate, Bishopsgate, and Aldgate; Moorgate was a medieval addition. Excavations at Newgate Street in 1909 revealed the plan of the Roman gateway, with its double roadway, and roadworks at Aldersgate in 1939 uncovered a mass of Roman masonry.

It is possible that Aldersgate, being set slightly askew to the line of the wall, was an afterthought by the Romans, and not the entrance of a major road as Newgate was.

Smithfield lay immediately outside the wall, unprotected, and was not built on. Instead, it was used as a rubbish dump and cemetery; a stone altar to the Roman god Mercury found at Farringdon Road, beside the bank of the old Fleet River, may have been a Mithraic shrine for the dead.

In A.D. 410, the Romans left Londinium. Fifth-century buckles from the belts of German mercenaries found at Smithfield confirm the considerable efforts to which the remaining Londoners went to defend their town against the invading hordes of Angles, Saxons and Jutes. Their defence was futile; the Roman town was overrun and abandoned in about A.D. 450.

Despite the desertion of Roman London, the city wall remained through the Dark Ages and was used as the foundations for its rebuilding when London was reoccupied by the Saxons, who added a V-shaped ditch twenty feet outside the perimeter. The city wall remained fixed on the Roman line throughout the Middle Ages, although in the thirteenth century it was extended to take in Black-friars. It was carefully maintained, the last repair being as late as 1476.

In the seventh and eighth centuries, resettlement was almost entirely within the walls. As the town grew, so the walls took on a greater importance, no longer purely military, but as the boundary of the city within which trade regulations, laws and curfews were enforced. At the gates, tolls and murage (a tax levied for the wall's upkeep) were collected. In Saxon times there was plenty of space and considerable areas within the wall remained undeveloped, but trade flourished and population grew, until inevitably the city wall became a straitjacket. Londoners began to look outside the walls to accommodate activities which required extensive space. The open, level ground beyond the walls between Newgate and Aldersgate proved ideal.

Smithfield was indeed originally a 'smooth field'. Stow, the great Elizabethan chronicler, records that at one time there was a large pond at Smithfield called 'Horsepoole', where citizens and travellers watered their animals. Later, however, the spring dried out and the

An imaginary rooftop view of 15th-century London Newgate and St. Sepulchre's tower at the bottom, Greyfriars and the Shambles market beyond. **Museum of London**

19

pond was filled in. Fagges Well, near present-day Charterhouse, also dried up in medieval times. The group of elm trees which stood at Smithfield was felled in the fifteenth century. From the high land, with its springs and elm trees, the ground fell quickly to the Fleet River (named after the Saxon 'fleot', meaning creek), bordered by marshy water meadows. The valley is still clearly visible today.

The Fleet River was a substantial stream. North of the Holborn bridge, up to which point it was tidal, there were watermills which gave Turnmill Street its name. Wooden piles from a watermill's weir were unearthed in 1855 when the foundations of Farringdon Road were being laid. From Newgate, the westward road descended steeply to the Fleet, down the present-day Snow Hill and crossed the river by a wooden bridge, climbing the other side of the valley to what is now High Holborn, which in the tenth century was a 'wide army street'. Holborn probably takes its name from the 'bourn' in the 'hollow'. Snow Hill was steep and treacherous for carts; it is still worth a gearchange on a modern bike. From Aldersgate, a small lane (Goswell Road) meandered to the village of Iseldon (Islington).

The greatest legacy to the present was the siting of the cattle market at Smithfield. Markets had been set up inside the city, mainly along the east-west axis of Cheapside, but there was no room here for an expanding cattle-market. Butchers' meat was the mark of a wealthy table; London's population was growing in numbers and wealth, and demanded a large cattle market.

As in many provincial market towns today, the cattle market was a once-a-week affair. William Fitzstephen, who was a clerk to Thomas à Becket, describes the market in 1174:

"A smooth field where every Friday there is a celebrated rendezvous of fine horses to be sold, and in another quarter are placed vendibles of the peasant, swine with their deep flanks, and cows and oxen of immense bulk."

Pens or folds were erected to contain the livestock; animals would have been driven up from the country several days before the market and kept there. As well as those trading in livestock – the farmers, drovers, horse dealers, and butchers – there were doubtless other pedlars selling their wares at the Friday market, keen to avoid the taxes that were levied at the city gates.

In many ways Smithfield was an ideal spot, close to, but removed from, the busy centre of London's traffic. London's population was small, and meat-eating was restricted by religious days of abstinence. It was possible to observe as many as 150 fish days in a year, leaving only 215 flesh days! When a charter for the market was granted in 1327, few could have imagined how the modest weekly market would expand in later years.

Slaughtered meat was sold inside the city in the butchers' quarter known as the Shambles. This ran along the present line of Newgate

Street, extending from the Newgate (which was near the junction with Giltspur Street) to St. Martin's-le-Grand. Originally, livestock bought at Smithfield were slaughtered in the Shambles, the waste being dumped in the Fleet. The stench of blood and entrails must have been horrific, particularly in summer. Until 1843 King Edward Street was known as Stinking Lane. The west end of Newgate Street was called Flesh Shambles and the east end, Bladder Street. In 1381, the city authorities not surprisingly banned slaughtering from the city, but the problem simply moved into the streets and houses of Smithfield, outside the city walls.

The lanes and roads leading to the market soon acquired predictable names – Cowcross, which still runs northwest to Turnmill Street, Cow Lane (now known as Smithfield Street), Cock Lane, Chick Lane, and Duck Lane (later Duke Street and now the north end of Little Britain). The open pens of the market and the lanes that converged on it soon were lined with inns, houses and tenements to serve the visitors to the market. By 1394, there were ninety-five commercial inns in the Smithfield area outside the walls. Smithfield thus became one of London's earliest suburbs. It was not long before the city authorities took steps to ensure that the 'liberties' also came within their jurisdiction.

Bars, or outer gates, were established in the twelfth century, and legalised in 1222. At Smithfield, the bars were sited at the bottom end of St. John's Street, immediately south of its junction with Cowcross Street. There were also bars at Holborn, Temple, and Spitalfields. The position of these bars is still the boundary of the modern City of London. The bars, with chains or wooden poles across the road, were control points for all travellers approaching the city, for collecting commercial dues, keeping out lepers, serfs and vagabonds. This must have been a tiresome duty, for in those days a serf who could prove he had lived in the city for a year and a day could gain his freedom.

Pressure on land within the city encouraged the establishment of religious houses outside the walls, where land was plentiful. Three of these were in the Smithfield area; the Priory and Hospital of St. Bartholomew, the Carthusian monastery known as The Charterhouse, and the Priory of St. John of Jerusalem. North of St. John's was St. Mary's Nunnery, Clerkenwell. The high ground and excellent water supply from springs and wells were ideal. All these institutions have a marvellous history and contribute to Smithfield today, and deserve their own chapters.

Inside the city wall, on the north side of Newgate Street, where the Post Office is now, the Greyfriars built their home in 1225, on land that had been hitherto left vacant because of the vile smell from the Shambles. The long-suffering Friars endured this worldly odour gladly, and their numbers grew rapidly until the Black Death. East of the Greyfriars was the College and church of St. Martin's-le-Grand,

founded in A.D. 700. The church bell signalled the evening curfew in the city, while the church had rights of sanctuary for criminals and debtors. Nothing remains today except the street name.

Parish churches sprung up all over the city. St. Sepulchre's, just outside Newgate, is first mentioned in 1137. The tower and south porch survive from the fifteenth century rebuilding, although heavy pinnacles were added in 1878. Parishioners at St. Sepulchre's could join a 'gild' contributing a farthing a week which provided fourteen pence a week in times of need and a decent funeral – medieval social security.

St. Botolph's, beside Aldersgate, was founded before 1290, and dedicated to the patron saint of travellers. Nothing of the medieval church is left. The land north of St. Botolph's was owned by the Dukes of Brittany, hence the naming of Little Britain. Fronting Aldersgate Street was the Bishop of London's 'inn', known as London House.

St. Andrew's, Holborn, on the west bank of the Fleet, was originally a Saxon wood church, rebuilt in stone first by the Normans, and then again in 1446. Only the interior of the present tower dates from the fifteenth century. The view from St. Andrew's must have been magnificent once; the Fleet River winding north towards the woods and

22 *St. Sepulchre's Church, in about 1800.*
The original 15th-century tower has
not yet been embellished by the
Victorians. **Museum of London**

heights of Highgate and Hampstead, and across the valley the city wall, with the church towers and spire of St. Paul's rising majestically above.

Across the road from St. Andrew's stood the palace of the Bishop of Ely. The Roman Catholic church of St. Etheldreda's, tucked away in Ely Place, is the sole survivor of the original fourteenth century 'inn', with its cloisters, gatehouse, banqueting hall, and commodious domestic buildings. The chapel with its fine traceried east window and crypt is well worth a visit. Being within the bishopric the inn was exempt from the control of the City, and enjoyed rights of sanctuary. Ely Place remains a private road today; the gates are locked at night and there is no entry without prior arrangement.

The spacious and well kept garden was much admired; in Shakespeare's *Richard III* this is noted by the Duke of Gloucester:

"My Lord of Ely, when I was last in Holborn, I saw good strawberries in your garden there; I do beseech you send for some of them."

North of the inn fertile market gardens, growing onions, leeks, garlic, parsley and cabbages, sloped down to the Fleet River.

Successive Bishops of Ely were powerful churchmen holding considerable political sway. Ely Palace became renowned for its lavish entertaining. Colossal feasts were held there, none greater than the five-day marathon in May, 1531, attended by Henry VIII, barons, ambassadors, and city aldermen. Stow painstakingly itemises the menu:—24 great beefs, 100 fat muttons, 51 veals, 34 porks, 91 pigs, 10 dozen capons, 14 dozen cocks, 37 dozen pigeons, 14 dozen swans, 340 dozen larks . . .

John of Gaunt, Duke of Lancaster and father of Henry IV, lived here after his palace at the Savoy had been burnt. His dying words at Ely Palace in 1399 were immortalised and embellished by Shakespeare in 'Richard II':

"This royal throne of kings, this sceptred isle . . .
This precious stone set in the silver sea . . .
This blessed plot, this earth, this realm, this England."

The wide space at Smithfield became a favourite place for tournaments and jousting by the nobility. Tournaments were very grand social occasions, important for diplomatic prestige as well as chivalric rivalry, and were held with great pomp and ceremony. Stow's description of the procession to Smithfield is picturesque:

"Knights well armed and mounted at the Tower, ryding from thence through that street west to Crede Lane, and so out at Ludgate towards Smithfield when they were there to turney, iust, or otherwise to shew activities before the King."

Stow recounts many famous tournaments; in 1362 on the first five days of May jousts were held, Edward III being present together with most of the nobility of England and France, as well as knights from

Spain, Cyprus and Armenia, seeking support against the Turks. It is likely that Chaucer, who was Clerk of the Works, supervised the building lists at Smithfield.

Smithfield was also used for more common sports – football, wrestling and archery all being popular – the latter encouraged for military reasons. Religious mystery plays were performed here and one play in 1409, retelling the story of the Creation, actually lasted eight days. In May, 1978, a revival of a fifteenth-century morality play was performed at the church of St. Bartholomew-the-Great, depicting the struggle between good and evil in the life of mankind. A nice idea, and not irrelevant to a modern audience.

However, the great event at Smithfield, lasting for three days every August, was Bartholomew Fair. It started in the reign of Henry II as a response to the growing cloth trade in London. Merchants from all over Europe travelled to the international cloth fair at Lendit (now St. Denis, Paris). Bartholomew Fair and the great Stourbridge Fair at Cambridge were the English equivalents where the clothiers and drapers bought their supplies for the following year. Other local merchandise was exchanged such as leather, horses, cheeses and trinkets, and many side shows and amusements, such as bull and bear baiting, took place besides the main business of the fair. It soon became one of London's most popular public holidays.

A more morbid use of the open space was for executions. There are early accounts of condemned men being drawn by the heels from the Tower to the Elms at Smithfield, and hanged. In 1305 William Wallace, who for thirty years had been a Scottish thorn in the English flesh, was captured, brought to London and put to death at Smithfield. A plaque on the outer wall of St. Bartholomew's Hospital praises his heroism – in Gaelic. Two years later his brother and two brothers of Robert Bruce also died here, as did Roger Mortimer, murderer of Edward II.

In 1381 the Peasants' Revolt, led by Wat Tyler, reached its climax at Smithfield. The uprising, which was sparked off by a new and crippling poll-tax,* had culminated in the capture of London, in itself one of the most extraordinary events in England's history. Following the sacking of St. John's Priory and the Savoy palace, and the murder of many dignitaries, the mob was confronted by William Walworth, the mayor, and the fourteen-year-old Richard II on the open ground at Smithfield. Wat Tyler was struck down and badly wounded in a scuffle with Walworth, and the rebels retreated to Clerkenwell. Shortly afterwards Tyler was dragged from his refuge in St. Bartholomew's church and beheaded. His head was taken to Clerkenwell and displayed before the remaining rabble, who dispersed quickly. So ended the revolt.

During the Middle Ages increasing numbers of people came to live in the liberty of Smithfield, for one reason or another. Prostitutes,

*Can a re-occurrence be expected in 1990?

The Burning of St. JOHN's MONASTRY near Smithfield, by Wat Tyler's Mob.

banned from soliciting within the city walls, were actively encouraged by the authorities to live in Cock Lane, which soon became famous for its brothels – London's first red-light district. 'Clarice of Cokkes Lane', who appears in Langland's *Piers Plowman* was no doubt a courtesan. Many of the women however were Flemish, unable to find alternative employment.

Smithfield, both inside and outside the bars, became a flourishing industrial area. Certain activities such as pottery, tanning, slaugh-

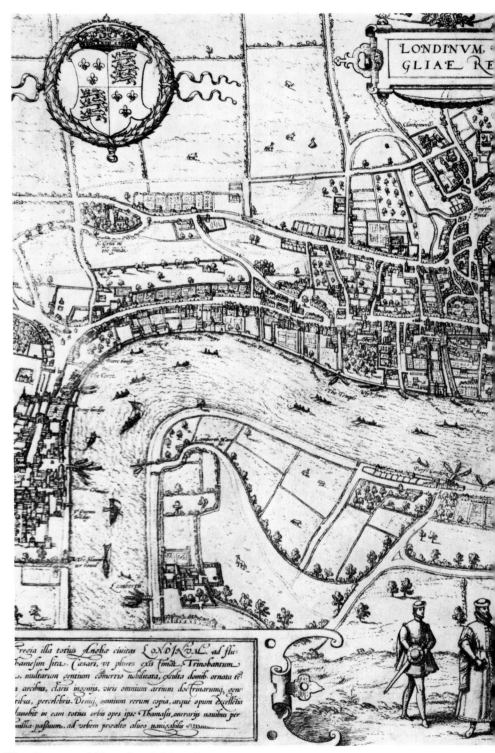

26 *Braun and Hogenberg's Map of London, 1590; "the most noble of cities".* **Museum of London**

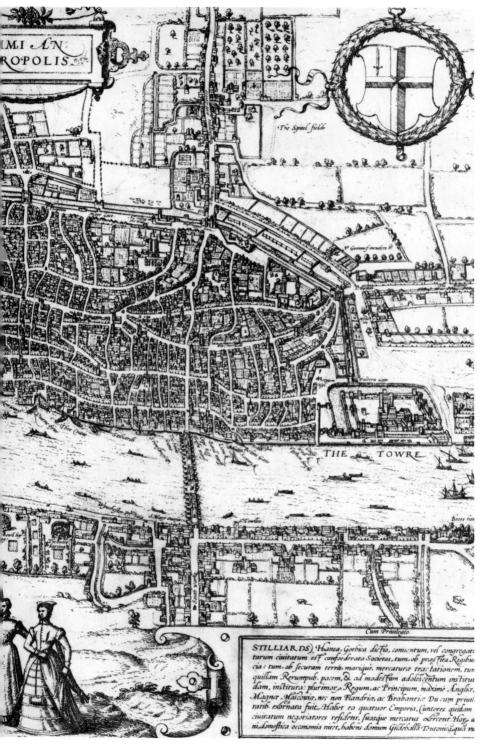

27

tering and dyeing were expelled from the city for environmental reasons. Tile and brick-making were attracted to the clay deposits in the Fleet valley. A medieval kiln was discovered near Farringdon Station during its construction, together with sample tiles decorated with the fleur-de-lys. A brick kiln continued to stand beside St. John's Gate in St. John's Lane until 1829.

Other industries came to escape the dues and controls of the City guilds which were compulsory within the city walls. In 1332 a certain John de Flaunden, a hosier, took the tenancy of a house in a lane immediately north of Cock Lane. It rapidly became an extremely fashionable street and retains the name Hosier Lane to this day. Giltspur Street possibly took its name from the spurriers who settled there. Sir John Falstaff in *Henry IV, Pt. II* went to Pye Corner in Giltspur Street to buy a saddle. Clearly the cattle market with its by-products, such as hides for leather, horns for buttons, hooves for glue, was instrumental in attracting industry.

Aldersgate was extended in the fourteenth century to form residential apartments and workshops over the gate. John Day, official printer to Henry VIII, had his rooms there, as did Ralph Strode, to whom *Troilus and Cressida* was dedicated by Chaucer. From the early 1200s Newgate, with its massive ironbound wooden gates, was used as a prison to house the worst and most dangerous felons and robbers.

The Black Death in 1348 ravaged London's population:

"And that year was the great pestilence of London, and through all England, and lasted from the feast of St. Michael unto the month of August next following, the year of our Lord 1349."   (*Gregory's Chronicle*)

The death toll reached 40% in the denser areas, and at its peak 200 corpses were buried each day in the mass graves at Greyfriars, Charterhouse and Bunhill Fields.

Despite heavy losses, the population outside the walls recovered quickly and was large enough by 1394 to justify the formation of a separate ward, Farringdon Without. By 1500, the Smithfield area was largely built up. The first printed map of London by Braun and Hogenberg in 1560 shows accurately the layout of streets and buildings in Smithfield. The similarity with the present-day street pattern is remarkable. St. John Street, St. John's Lane, Peters Lane, Cowcross Street and Turnmill Street were already lined with lath and plaster buildings. North of Aldersgate, Goswell Road was "replenished with small tenements, cottages, and alleys, gardens, banqueting houses and bowling places" (Stow). Long Lane, the "lane truly called long", connected Goswell Road and the market. Cock Lane, Hosier Lane, Cloth Fair, and the frontage facing the market were crammed with narrow three- and four-storeyed houses and inns, the upper floors projecting as jetties overshadowing the streets.

Fitzstephen had considered London to be "the most noble of cities", "a pleasant, merry place". Foreign visitors commented on the flocks of crows, rooks, kites and jackdaws in the sky, and admired the fine churches and schools. Yet by the end of the fifteenth century it is hard to imagine medieval Smithfield in such glowing terms, with its livestock, executions, prostitutes, prisons, and rubbish dumped in the ditch beside the wall.

THE TUDORS TO THE GEORGES

During the next 300 years, Smithfield continued to develop on similar lines. The institutions and activities which had sprung up in the Middle Ages flourished with only a few exceptions.

In the sixteenth century London's population grew rapidly, reflecting the comparative prosperity and stability of the time. Serious overcrowding resulted and every piece of land inside the bars became used, and beyond the bars London's suburbs spread. John Stow saw dramatic changes during his life. By the time he died, as an octogenarian in 1605, the fields he had played in as a boy were built over.

The open meadows and gardens beside the Fleet River became a labyrinth of lanes, alleys and courtyards, with poorer ramshackle houses hidden away behind smarter properties facing the street. Control on building was minimal. In 1597 it was discovered that thirty tenements and twelve thatched cottages had been built on a public rubbish dump in Chick Lane, completely unknown to the authorities.

Smithfield attracted many of the more unfortunate sections of the community; Irish immigrants, labourers, lodgers, prostitutes, beggars, vagabonds and criminals. Daniel Defoe in 1709 divided the social classes into seven groups. Of the bottom two, "The poor, that fare hard," and, "The miserable, that really pinch and suffer want", Smithfield had more than its fair share. The jumble of alleys on either side of the Fleet was soon a notorious 'rookery', as slums were known in the eighteenth century, a rabbit warren of insalubrious hovels where the population was always shifting and an area respectable people would avoid.

Disease and outbreaks of plague were common. By 1600 the Fleet River was little more than an open sewer and a constant threat to health. This was partly an administrative blunder; the city authorities had no jurisdiction beyond the bars and could not force the Middlesex justices to clean the river above the Holborn bridge: nor could they prevent the spread of pollution downstream. Swift provides a lurid description:

"Now from all parts the swelling kennels flow,

30 *The Fat Boy of Pye Corner marks the furthest extent of the Great Fire of London. Perhaps a brass monkey would be more appropriate!*
Theo Bergström

And bear their trophies with them as they go;
Filth of all hues and odours seems to tell
What street they sail'd from by their sight and smell,
They, as each torrent drives its rapid force,
From Smithfield to St. 'Pulchre's shape their course,
And in huge confluence joins at Snowhill ridge,
Fall from the Conduit prone to Holborn Bridge;
Sweepings from butchers' stalls, dung, guts and blood,
Drown'd puppies, stinking sprats, all drench'd in mud,
Dead cats, and turnip tops, come tumbling down the flood."

Smithfield's population must have been savaged by the Great Plague of 1665, when 110,000 people died in London. Mass burial pits were dug in the fields north of Smithfield and Clerkenwell. Pepys' Diary records in 31st August, 1665, "in the City died this week 7,496 and of them 6,102 of the Plague." The plague pits still survive; nearly every park or playground in Finsbury is an old burial ground.

Most buildings were still timber with lath and plaster. The gatehouse to St. Bartholomew's churchyard is one of the few surviving examples in London of this type of building. There are only about twenty Tudor or pre-Tudor buildings left in the whole of London, and many of these are in the Smithfield area; the wooden gatehouse mentioned above, the stone-built Charterhouse and St. John's Gate, St. Bartholomew-the-Great, St. Etheldreda's, and the tower of St. Bartholomew-the-Less. The reason for this scarcity today was the Great Fire of London.

It broke out on 2nd September, 1666, and spread west towards the Temple. By the time it was halted at Smithfield on 6th September four-fifths of the city, including 88 churches and 13,200 houses, were destroyed. Smithfield was saved by the wall and its ditch, and by a fluke change of wind when the fire threatened to engulf Holborn. The furthest extent of the fire was the corner of Giltspur Street and Cock Lane, known as Pye Corner, to this day marked by a small gilt statue of a cupid-like boy mounted on the wall. The Fat Boy of Pye Corner was supposedly a warning against the gluttony and avarice which moralists and budding soothsayers claimed had brought about the Fire in the first place.

Wenceslaus Hollar's *Exact Surveigh of Burnt London*, in 1667, clearly shows the extent of the Fire. St. Sepulchre's Church, Newgate and its prison, and Holborn bridge were destroyed. Had it not been for the city wall and its ditch, the church of St. Bartholomew would probably be a Wren church today. Nos. 41–2 Cloth Fair are two rare, surviving examples of pre-Fire Jacobean houses, with their two-storeyed rectangular wooden bay windows, beautifully restored by Seely and Paget. After the Fire, strict controls were placed on inflammable projecting woodwork.

While Smithfield's escape may please historians and conservation-

The Prospect of this Citty as it appeared from the opposite Southwarke side in the fire time.

Hatton Garden

Smith Field

Aldersgate

Libertie
of S Mar
tins le
Grand

Paules Churchyard

Ludgate

Bridewell

Fleet Street

Thames Street

a Scale of Feet.

Published with the description of the Wards by the care Industrie
and Charge of Nathaniel Brooke Stationer, and are to be Sould
at his shop at the Angell in the second Yard of Gresham Colledge
leading from Byshopsgate street.

THE   R I V E R

PUBLICATION No. 104 replacing Nos. 22 & 26.

London Topographical Society   9 Rivercourt Road   London W6

HOLLAR'S "EXACT SU

32 Wenceslaus Hollar's map of London,
    showing the area devastated by the
    Fire. The medieval wall saved
    Smithfield's streets and buildings.
    Museum of London

TY OF LONDON, 1667

ists, it meant at the time that the slums and rookeries remained, congested and disease-ridden. Defoe lamented in 1722 that the rookeries were in the same condition as they were before the Fire.

The livestock market at Smithfield grew with London's population. By 1725 London was consuming 60,000 cattle, 70,000 sheep and 239,000 pigs each year. Animals were driven enormous distances from the country to Smithfield for sale and slaughter; sheep from Lincoln, Norfolk and the West Country, cattle from Wales and Scotland.

The journey from Scotland was a long and exacting one. Cows on Skye had to swim the first part of their 550 mile journey to London! Cattle from all over Scotland were collected together at great fairs, the largest of which was the Falkirk Tryst. Here the cattle were transferred to 'jobbers' or dealers, gathered into huge herds, each up to a thousand beasts, and driven south.

The drovers were highly paid, due reward for their onerous responsibility. The Highland drover, "a child amongst flocks but a prince amongst herds", received the admiration of Sir Walter Scott:

> "It affords exercise for all their habits of patient endurance and active exertion. They are required to know perfectly the drove-roads, which lie over the wildest parts of the country, and to avoid as much as possible the highways, which destroy the feet of the bullocks, and the turnpikes, which annoy the spirit of the drover; whereas, in the broad green or gray track which leads across the pathless moor, the herd not only move at ease and without taxation, but if they mind their business may pick up a mouthful of food by the way. At night the drovers usually sleep along with their cattle, let the weather be what it will; and many of these hardy men do not once rest under a roof during a journey on foot from Lochaber to Lincolnshire."

The journey south took about three weeks, and frequently the cattle were taken via Lincolnshire, Norfolk or Suffolk, for fattening before finally being driven to Smithfield market for sale.

Other animals had to endure similar hardship. Huge droves of turkeys and geese marched up to eighty miles from Norfolk and Suffolk villages, their feet wrapped in little cloth shoes! The great drovers' roads usually by-passed towns and villages, for obvious reasons, and can still be traced today, as tracks or fragments of minor roads. Nearer London the Holloway Road and the Archway Road, skirting Highgate Village, were main drovers' highways from the north.

At Islington all available pasture, not already under dairy cows, was used for fattening animals before they were escorted to Smithfield by the London drovers, distinguished by their special arm badges issued by the City Corporation. Huge convoys of horses drawing heavy broad-wheeled wagons brought hay from the country as

supplementary fodder. The country drovers were thus relieved of their duties at Islington and the animals entrusted to an official salesmen's drover for the final descent down the twisting length of St. John Street, through the Smithfield Bars and to their allotted place in the market. When an animal was sold, the salesman cut off a small portion of hair from the hide as a mark. A third set of drovers, employed by the butchers, navigated the animals through the busy city streets to the slaughterhouses. The street drover had a hard life, struggling continuously against obstacles. In the eighteenth century an amusing essay appeared on *The Graces and Anxieties of Pig Driving . . . .* "a pig is sluggish, obstinate, opinionate, not very social and has no desire of seeing foreign parts. Think of him in a multitude, forced to travel, and wondering what the devil it is that drives him! Judge by this of the talent of his drover!"

By the nineteenth century, there were about one hundred master drovers who ran the market and hired other men. The remaining responsibility rested with the salesmen, to whom the cattle owner consigned his stock. The salesmen examined the stock and decided which to expose for sale that morning, depending on price and demand. A compromise had to be struck between selling too cheaply and stagnating the market. Salesmen were paid on commission and seven or eight banking houses sprang up around the market to handle all the financial transactions.

In 1614, the market was paved and drained for the first time and extended considerably up towards The Charterhouse. Although tolls had been collected since 1400, the Corporation formalised this by Royal Charter in 1638. The improved Smithfield was described as "a most capacious market for black cattle, sheep, horses, hay and straw, with pens or folds, so called of sheep there parted and penned up to be

Eighteenth-century Smithfield "a most capacious market". The large corner tavern is the Bishop's Finger public house today. **G.L.C.**

sold on market days." In fact there were pens and rails for about 4,000 cattle, sheep and pigs for which dues were payable. By the seventeenth century, the market was operating several days a week. Monday morning was the busiest (as strangely it still is today). Throughout the Sunday night a great stream of well-fattened animals plodded down St. John Street from the fields and lairs of Islington. A fine sight it must have been, but any romantic view must be tempered by the congestion, filth and smell, which was only to get worse as the trade of the market increased. The flies, blood and dung are best viewed from the safety of intervening centuries!

Up to the early eighteenth century, there had always been difficulties in fattening livestock. Sheep and cattle were fed on stubble, heaths and commons, and animals arriving at Smithfield were emaciated after a long journey. With no root crops or grasses for winter fodder most animals were killed at the end of the summer grass, and Smithfield market virtually ceased trading during the winter.

The agricultural revolution in the eighteenth century brought tremendous change. By 1795 the average weight of carcases at the market was twice that of 1710. With new winter feeds, the wholesale slaughter of stock at the end of autumn stopped, and the market operated all year. For the first time fresh beef and mutton were available in winter, instead of salted meat. Scurvy and other skin diseases which had been common even in aristocratic families (such as the Verneys in the seventeenth century) became rare even among the poor. Smithfield grew from strength to strength, but clearly could not do so indefinitely on a restricted site.

Bartholomew Fair continued to prosper, and there was also a May Fair. Increasingly the side shows took over from the serious business of trading – jugglers, acrobats, ballad mongers, gingerbread sellers, pick-pockets and tricksters prospered. Ben Jonson's *Bartholomew Fair* describes the coarse buffoonery of the early seventeenth century. Like many others, Pepys came just to have a good time and marvel at the curiosities, such as "the Wonder of Nature" – "a sixteen-year-old girl, only twelve inches tall who could sing and whistle!" Bartholomew 'babies', small wooden dolls bought at the fair, were also popular.

Despite the growth of theatre, pleasure gardens and more civilised pursuits, many entertainments remained extremely barbaric – prize fighting with bare fists, badger baiting, and bizarre contests between battling women or between a man and a dog. Such brutality was usually an excuse for betting. Cock fighting became the most popular gaming sport, appealing to all classes, until it was banned in 1849. Permanent cock-pits were established, a famous one being Hockley-in-the-Hole at Clerkenwell. Boswell's first view of a cock fight shocked him; looking for sympathy among the audience, "I could not

observe the smallest relenting sign in any countenance."

In 1762 the Cock Lane Ghost which haunted No. 33 Cock Lane aroused much excitement. Crowds of people, including Joshua Reynolds, Goldsmith, Dr. Johnson and Horace Walpole, flocked to hear the ghost of 'Scratching Fanny'. It was eventually exposed as a fraud, but not before all the taverns in the area had made a fortune from the unexpected trade.

Prostitution continued to flourish in the Cock Lane area: "at the approach of night they sally forth from their homes . . . . low taverns serve them as a retreat to receive their gallants." Some of the Smithfield whores became well known; Mrs. Martha King, "a little fat

An 18th-century predecessor of the big
wheel at Bartholomew Fair.
Finsbury Library

woman, known last winter by her velvet gown and petticoat"; Mrs. Elizabeth Brown, "a very fine woman, who has been a dealer in cullies ever since she was fifteen; modest and pleasant enough, till after the third bottle", and Mrs. Sarah Farmer, "a great two-handed strapper, having no charms either in person or humour". In reality many girls were very young or "half eaten up with the Foul Distemper".

An even greater scourge in the eighteenth century was gin or 'geneva', particularly among the poor. Originally promoted to reduce imports of French brandy, gin was distilled openly without interference. The product was crude, fiery and cheaper than meths today. The streets and alleys north of Ely Place, beside the Fleet, became a notorious den of excessive gin-drinking, the setting of Hogarth's *Gin Lane*. Hogarth, born in 1697 at No. 58 Bartholomew Close, was brought up surrounded by the seamier side of Smithfield life. His father had mixed fortunes, running a school, a coffee house and ending up in a debtors prison. Hogarth started as an engraver's apprentice and his etchings and sketches soon became respected for their sharp social comment. *Gin Lane* may well have hastened the Act of 1751 which banned unlicensed gin distilling, although even after 1751 over 15% of all adult deaths in the neighbourhood were still attributed to excessive spirit drinking. Apothecaries continued to be able to sell spirits as medicine and the demand for 'gripe and cholic waters' was prodigious. Taverns continued to sell gin liquors,

Hogarth's satirical portrayal of the Cockpit. He clearly shared Boswell's dislike of the cruelty and wild gambling. **British Museum**

but now disguised in name and appearance – 'sangaree', 'tow-row', 'cuckold's comfort', 'ladies' delight', and 'parliament gin'. Antagonists of alcoholism saw coffee as the great salvation. "No man is ever tempted to get drunk upon coffee or to lower himself below the level of brutes." Coffee houses were seen as "places conducive to sobriety and general intelligence".

Smithfield developed further as a place for punishing crime. In the sixteenth century it was famous for its 'Fires', the burnings of religious martyrs. In 1510 the Bishop of London had heretics burnt at Smithfield, but worse was to come. During the brief reign of Queen Mary, when the Catholic faith was re-established, over 200 Protestants died at Smithfield. These included John Rogers, vicar of St. Sepulchre's, John Aston, who was found illegally eating pork during Lent at his house in Charterhouse Lane, and John Rough, close friend of John Knox, the Scottish reformer, who was discovered holding a

Gin Lane 1751. Smithfield born and bred, Hogarth had only to look at the nearby rookeries to find inspiration for this famous etching. **British Museum**

40 *The corner of Snow Hill and Cock
Lane, where John Bunyan died, and
site of the Saracen's Head Inn.
St. Sepulchre's and the Old Bailey
behind.* **Theo Bergström**

Protestant service in a back room of the Saracen's Head Inn on the corner of Snow Hill and Cock Lane. The victims were burnt facing the west door of St. Bartholomew's Church. When Elizabeth came to the throne in 1558, it was the turn of unrepenting Catholics. A plaque on the hospital wall commemorates 'the noble army of martyrs'.

Newgate prison, extended and rebuilt in 1420 with money left by Dick Whittington, continued to house London's worst criminals. Conditions in the prison deteriorated to an appalling degree in the eighteenth century, with chronic overcrowding, contaminated water, poor ventilation and no segregation of prisoners. Food, candles and privacy had to be bought from the corrupt turnkeys. Gaol-fever, a virulent form of typhoid, was rampant. Judges in the Old Bailey, which was built next to the prison in 1539, wore nosegays of sweet-smelling herbs, but despite this precaution many judges and jurors caught the fever. The ineffectual nosegays are still carried by judges on the opening day of sessions as a reminder.

Newgate was considered to be impregnable; Jack Sheppard's escape from the death cell earned him immortality, even though he was recaptured and hanged. Ben Jonson, Christopher Marlowe, and Daniel Defoe all did time in Newgate for various suspected offences, and fortunately survived to tell the tale. Minor offenders either served a sentence or were flogged at the whipping post. This extremely nasty device is now exhibited in the Museum of London.

More serious criminals were, until 1783, taken to Tyburn gallows, near Marble Arch. The long journey by open cart was interrupted outside St. Sepulchre's, where the great bell was rung – the 'bells of Old Bailey' referred to in the nursery rhyme with its macabre undertones. A handbell, now in the church, was rung outside the condemned man's cell the previous night and a verse recited:

"All you that in the condemned hole do lie,
Prepare you for tomorrow you shall die.
Watch all and pray; the hour is drawing near
That you before the Almighty must appear.
Examine well yourselves, in time repent,
That you may not to eternal flames be sent,
And when St. Sepulchre's bell in the morning tolls
The Lord have mercy on your souls."

Hangings at Tyburn were eagerly awaited public holidays and attracted huge ghoulish crowds. In those days, Tyburn was well out in the country and people relished the prospect of a trip along the Oxford Road (what is now Oxford Street) and a good day's entertainment. Crowds thronged the route along Snow Hill and Holborn to cheer or boo the victim. Popular highwaymen were toasted like heroes with beer or gin; notorious thugs and informers, such as Jonathan Wild, were pelted with rotten vegetables and dung. The government had originally hoped that public executions would be a sobering deterrent, but by 1783 the festivities had become so wild that executions at Tyburn were abolished and transferred to the yard of Newgate prison. Crowds still flocked to Newgate, however, particularly to see a famous criminal die, such as Thistlewood and the Cato Street conspirators in 1820. Gruesome iron cages were used to display corpses in Newgate Street.

In 1770, the old prison was demolished and rebuilt by George Dance who was influenced by the Italian architect, Piranesi. Burnt down in the Gordon Riots in 1780, it was immediately repaired. The new prison, with its sombre, fortress-like facade, had three sections; male felons, female felons, and debtors. The blank walls were rusticated, rather like those of the Bank of England. Huge leg irons and fetters hung over the entrance as grim ornament. When the prison was finally demolished in 1902 the massive iron bolts, locks and cell doors were sold as souvenirs.

In addition to Newgate, a small prison or compter for drunkards and debtors stood in Giltspur Street, where the Post Office yard is now. In 1612 a sessions house was built at the south end of St. John Street, in the middle of the road where the public conveniences are today. Hick's Hall was used by the Middlesex justices, and in 1660 the twenty-nine regicides who had tried Charles I were themselves condemned there. Bodies of dead criminals were dissected in a back room, often by surgeons from St. Bartholomew's Hospital as practice. In 1777 a new sessions house was built at Clerkenwell Green and

42 *Newgate Gaol, supposedly impregnable, under attack during the Gordon Riots of 1780.*
Museum of London

Hick's Hall was demolished. The new sessions house still stands at the west end of Clerkenwell Green, magnificently restored over the last few years by the Freemasons.

The rookeries beside the Fleet became a favourite haunt for many criminals, as a hiding place and depository. In the eighteenth century there were cases of brazen highwaymen robbing coaches in Holborn. The Red Lion tavern in Chick Lane was a notorious lodging-house for thieves and footpads from 1750. "It has all the conveniences of a hiding place, with concealed means of escape – in dark closets, sliding panels, and secret recesses, and by as many trap doors as in the stage of a theatre. By passing down one of these traps the pursued could evade the vigilance of the 'police' by getting through a window and crossing the Fleet Ditch over a plank which was kept at hand and afterwards drawn into the opposite house. The pursued might then pass into Black Boy Alley and thereby get into Cowcross, and the knot of courts and alleys in that neighbourhood." Some men eluded capture for years despite repeated searches. The slums of the Fleet were unrivalled as a breeding ground for vice, crime and poverty. Thos. H. Shepherd's sketch summarises the squalor. In the foreground a group of rag gatherers assess their day's spoils, while the brick building behind is part of the infamous Red Lion Inn.

Despite this dismal picture of crime, drunkenness and suffering, there had been some changes for the better. Between 1536 and 1540 Henry VIII had dissolved the monasteries which, in turn, had provided space for new building. On the site of Greyfriars, Edward VI founded Christ's Hospital in 1552 as a charitable school for 300 poor boys and orphans. Their distinctive uniform earned them the nick-

name of 'bluecoat boys'. Samuel Taylor Coleridge and Charles Lamb attended the school. On the wall of the watchhouse in Giltspur Street, erected in 1791 and restored after 1941, is a bust and inscription to Lamb: "perhaps the most loved name in English literature who was a bluecoat boy here for seven years". Charles Lamb later lived in Colebrooke Row, Islington, in a house which made him feel "like a lord". The school and its church were engulfed in the Fire, but rebuilt by Sir Christopher Wren. Christchurch was gutted in the Second World War and has not been restored. The tower remains, one of Wren's finest, but unbelievably the east end of the church was demolished by the City Corporation to widen the road – an act of myopic insensitivity.

The College and church of St. Martin's-le-Grand were pulled down in 1538. Several other religious houses were taken over as noblemen's homes; the Aylesbury's at St. John's Priory and the Norfolk's at The Charterhouse. Lord Berkeley built his London residence in St. John's Lane and Northumberland extended his house in St. Martin's-le-Grand.

St. Sepulchre's was badly damaged in the Fire and largely rebuilt in 1670. It is a roomy, barn-like church with no division between nave and chancel. Refurnishing included the organ and case by Renatus Harris and the beautiful reredos. Henry Wood, founder of Promenade concerts, is buried there, and a memorial exists to Dame Nellie Melba, after whom peach melba is named. The side chapel is dedicated to musicians, and musicologists can spend an absorbing hour identifying the musical quotes embroidered on the hassocks. Behind

44   *Inside the Red Lion Inn, depicted by*
      Hogarth. Pickpockets sort their spoils.
      The body of an unfortunate victim is
      disposed of. **Finsbury Library**

the church a row of almshouses, Snow Hill Court, was built, now used as offices. St. Sepulchre's graveyard was originally just south of Cowcross Street.

St. Andrew's, Holborn, escaped the Fire, but being dilapidated the opportunity was grasped to commission Wren to rebuild in 1686. This was his largest parish church, a superb example of his finest renaissance style, and incorporated the fifteenth-century tower. The organ with its elaborate case was donated by Handel in 1750. Dickens' David Copperfield timed his meetings with Agnes by the clock on the tower.

St. Botolph's was totally rebuilt in 1788 by Nathaniel Wright. The scale is charmingly modest, with an elegant Venetian east window and small west tower surmounted by a wooden bellcote. The eighteenth-century interior is intact, with dark wood galleries, pews and pulpit, and a fine moulded Wedgwood-blue ceiling. There are also some earlier Elizabethan monuments including a brass to Anne Packington, who died in 1563. Thomas Hood, the poet, was married here in 1825.

One of the church windows depicts John Wesley preaching at nearby Moorfields. Wesley received his evangelical conversion* on 24th May, 1738, in a meeting room at No. 28 Aldersgate Street, his brother Charles having been converted three days earlier at the house of John Bray, 12 Little Britain. Wesley preached to large congregations at St. Bartholomew's where "deep attention sat on every face". Another great religious reformer, John Bunyan, collapsed and died in Smithfield at the corner of Snow Hill and Cock

Beside the Red Lion Inn flowed the Fleet River, little more than an open sewer. In the foreground a family of rag gatherers. **British Museum**

*A splendid statue celebrating Wesley's conversion now stands in the approach to the Museum of London.

45

Lane on one of his infrequent visits to London, and was buried in Bunhill Fields nearby.

John Milton had even stronger ties with the area. Between 1639 and 1645 he lived in Maidenhead Court, which was off Aldersgate Street, in a "pretty garden-house". Here he wrote his treatise on divorce, prompted by his wife's current infidelity. In the first few months of the Restoration, Milton went into hiding in Bartholomew Close, but from 1661 he resided again in Aldersgate Street, where he wrote *Paradise Lost*.

46   *John Wesley. Part of an extraordinary 19th-century portrait. Each line comprises minute lettering giving a prose account of Wesley's life!*
The Charterhouse

The enormous growth in population and prosperity in the eighteenth century encouraged redevelopment in the Smithfield area, particularly in the more respectable streets. Charterhouse Square became a fashionable address, "neat and comely", and was surrounded on four sides by elegant terraced houses, built to meet new regulations. Nos. 4, 5 and 17 Charterhouse Square are fine examples of four-storey houses built in about 1716, with multi-coloured stock bricks with red dressings and rusticated quoins, flush frame windows and rich wooden doorcases. Nos. 12, 13, 14 and 22 are later eighteenth century.

The land between Turnmill Street and St. John's Lane, previously occupied by Lord Berkeley's house and a maze of courts and gardens, was developed in 1720, together with St. John's Square, by Simon Michell, a wealthy local magistrate. A few old alleys survive – Broad Yard, Faulkners Alley, White Horse Alley,* and Passing Alley – a Victorian corruption of something less polite! The rest disappeared with the building of Red Lion Street, Berkeley Street, and George Court (known today as Britton Street, Briset Street and Albion Place respectively). Large private houses were built for well-off city merchants, such as Thomas Britton, a coal merchant, who held musical evenings at his house† at which Handel often played the keyboard and where even a stray duchess or two were sometimes seen.

A substantial number of these Georgian houses survive – Nos. 27–32 and 54–59 Britton Street, Nos. 49–52 St. John's Square, Nos. 80–88 St. John Street and Nos. 43–45 Cloth Fair – though hardly any are still in domestic use. Often shop-fronts or extensions have been added and original panelling, fireplaces, staircases and glazing bars

Charterhouse Square, looking south. Today's mighty plane trees result from this careful 18th-century planting.
Museum of London

*Sadly, White Horse Alley was cleared away in 1989 for redevelopment.
† In Jerusalem Passage.

48   *Only the cars betray the date – 1930.*
Ely Place, built in 1770, remains a
secluded, unchanging corner in a
hectic part of London.   **G.L.C.**

ruthlessly removed in 'modernisation'.

In the eighteenth century the remnants of Ely Palace, except the chapel, were demolished and redeveloped under the speculative lease system. In the sixteenth century most of the gardens had been sold to Sir Christopher Hatton. The trunk of a cherry tree which marked the boundary between the bishop's garden and Hatton's garden still stands in the bar of the Mitre Tavern, which is tucked out of sight in the passageway from Hatton Garden to Ely Place. Dating from 1546, the pub was rebuilt in 1770. At this time Ely Place, a secluded row of houses, and Hatton Garden were laid out. William Cowper, the poet, studied law with a solicitor in Ely Place until it depressed him so much that he left London on the verge of madness!

In the Little Britain area, London House was levelled in 1766 and a new pattern of courts imposed – Albion Buildings, Montague Court, Cox's Court and Cross Keys Square – all of which are due shortly to be swept away for redevelopment.* Little Britain (then Duck Lane or Duke Street) was famous for its booksellers and printers. Pepys was a frequent visitor "to buy books and to kiss the pretty wife of a bookseller"! The *Daily Courant*, England's first newspaper, and the *Spectator* were originally printed here. Benjamin Franklin had lodgings in Little Britain in 1725, for which he paid 1s 6d a week, while working as a printer's journeyman.

By the time Horwood produced his map of London, Westminster and Southwark in 1799, parts of Smithfield had changed considerably since the Fire, although most streets retained their medieval lines. Horwood's map is extremely detailed and accurate, and makes an interesting comparison with the modern 1:1250 ordnance survey map. By then the city walls and gates had disappeared. Both Newgate and Aldersgate had been repaired after the Fire, but they became such a bottleneck for traffic that an Act of Parliament was passed enabling their demolition in 1761.

Traffic had become a serious problem:

"There be very few gentlemen of any account who have not their own coaches, so as the streets of London are almost stopped up with them."

"Even people who have but a jackass will have a cart."

"In every street, carts and coaches make such a thundering as if the world ran upon wheels."

The increase in numbers, speed and size, was a similar problem to that caused by the juggernaut today.

In 1757 Marylebone and Euston Road were laid out as the 'new road', designed to take the cattle travelling to Smithfield – London's first by-pass. Until 1737 pavements were non-existent; bollards were the first attempt to control the surge of traffic and protect pedestrians, but of course did not stop the constant spattering of mud and manure. Steps were also taken to improve street lighting which had

*This has now been completed: there was no reprieve.

*St. John's Path, and the back of
Britton Street, warts and all. Nearly
all these houses are now workshops or
offices.* **Theo Bergström**

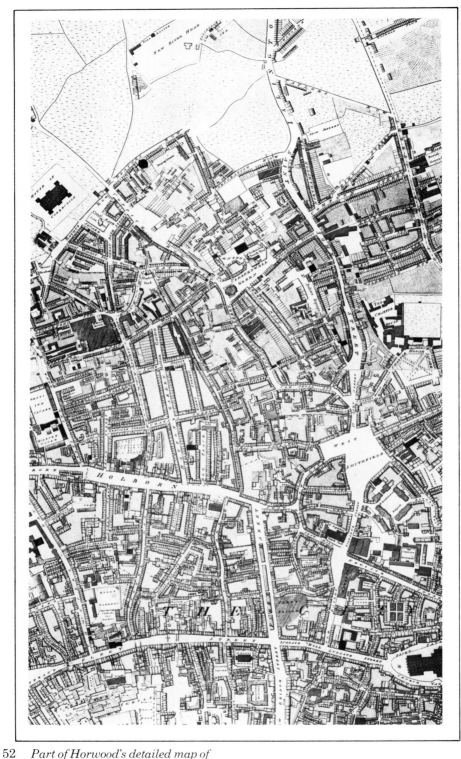

52   *Part of Horwood's detailed map of London, Westminster and Southwark, 1799. Every house is shown with painstaking care.* **Museum of London**

been totally absent in the back streets. No wonder the nightwatch-men and constables had a hopeless struggle trying to enforce law and order.

One of the greatest achievements was the covering of the Fleet River, first up as far as the Holborn bridge in 1747. The culvert was extended in 1755. A long arcaded market was built on the newly available space to house the general retail market of Cheapside and the Shambles.

Despite these improvements, much of Smithfield remained an appalling slum – "a hotch-potch of half-moon and serpentine narrow streets, close, dismal, long lanes, stinking alleys, dark, gloomy courts and suffocating yards" (*The Times*). Smithfield no longer had the advantage of being on the edge of London, with green fields beyond. The lane north of Turnmill Street, now part of Farringdon Road, was once known as Town's End. By 1820 more fashionable suburbs were spreading north and west – Clerkenwell, Amwell, Barnsbury, Bloomsbury, Covent Garden, Westminster, Camden Town. Within Smithfield an enormous legacy of filth and squalor was left for the Victorians to deal with.

VICTORIAN IMPROVEMENTS

Victorian England saw the awakening of a new con-sciousness and concern for utilitarian improvements. Led by philanthropic and economic reformers, public out-rage grew at the disease and squalor in London's poorer districts, and was latched onto by politicians. Disraeli, who incidentally had been baptised at St. Andrew's Holborn in 1817, described the Thames in 1858 as "a Stygian pool, reeking with ineff-able and intolerable horrors". Frederick Engels commented in 1844, "there are hundreds and thousands of alleys and courts lined with houses too bad for anyone to live in who can still spend anything whatsoever upon a dwelling fit for human beings. Close to the splen-did houses of the rich such a lurking place of the bitterest poverty may often be found."

The rookeries of the Fleet valley were as bad as any in London. Overcrowding and death rates continued to get worse in the first half of the nineteenth century. The population of Clerkenwell, for example, trebled between 1801 and 1861. In Farringdon and Cler-kenwell, people were living at densities of over 230 to the acre, while 28 out of every 1,000 people died each year. Most people, if they had a job, worked as labourers or porters, or in sweatshop employment, such as making clothes or artificial flowers. Saffron Hill and Cler-kenwell became a ghetto for Italian immigrants, a 'little Italy'. St. Peter's Italian Church in Back Hill, St. Catherine Laboure Roman Catholic primary school in Herbal Hill and the cluster of Italian cafes still betray an Italian flavour in the area.

Although stricter sanitary and building laws were introduced, they were not always properly enforced. Just as the police were reluctant to patrol the maze of back alleys, so sanitary officers were even more timid, and the slums remained an undisturbed breeding ground for fever and pestilence, as well as a mugger's paradise. The solution was to sweep the slums away, although, as Marx pointed out, this often only crowded the poor even more closely in another quarter. 'Model dwellings' such as the Peabody estates were built to provide alternative accommodation, but the cheap rents were still beyond many incomes.

By the end of the eighteenth century, Smithfield market was reaching saturation point – the inevitable result of an expanding population, an increase in meat-eating, and a confined market site. During the year of 1810 approximately 140,000 cattle and 1 million sheep were sold at Smithfield; by 1828 this had grown to 150,000 cattle and 1½ million sheep and by 1853 to 277,000 cattle and 1,600,000 sheep.

The 'Great Day' at Smithfield was the most stupendous event, held just before Christmas each year when the Christmas Dinner was bought. By daybreak on the Monday morning 30,000 animals were crammed into the four or five acre space. All round the market animals encroached on space rightfully belonging to shopkeeping traffic. Giltspur Street, Long Lane, Little Britain, St. John Street and Hosier Lane were all invaded. Here are the words of a contemporary witness:

"It presented an agitated sea of brute life. Drovers were hurrying hither and thither, carrying flaming torches in their hands, and arranging the cattle in rings and sheep in pens. The poor cattle could not, from very want of room, be tied up in rows, in quiet side-by-side brotherhood; large numbers were separated into groups of about twenty each, called rings, in which all the animals stood together with their heads towards a common centre. In one place was a group of brown-coated Devons; in a second a group of bulky Herefords; here and there were the favourite short-horns; a mass of black Scotch cattle diversified the picture in one spot, a cargo of Holsteiners in another, and a small number of rugged-coated monstrously-horned Spanish cattle in a third. The sheep, wedged up in dense masses in pens wholly beyond the reach of water, bleated away their wretched hours in the north-east corner of the market; while the pigs, large bacon hogs, small neat porkers and sucking pigs, squeaked lustily in the north-west. Here, at one place, was an ox towering over all the rest, and having the reputation of weighing 300 stones; and there, at another spot, was a pig of 40 score, a weight at least equal to that of an average Smithfield ox. The salesmen,

drovers and butchers, many of them booted to the thighs, dashed in amongst the dense masses, and after incredible difficulties separated the animals sufficiently to enable the butchers to inspect them before purchasing. Thus engaged, it seemed to others scarcely conceivable that those men could escape injuries from horns and hoofs, especially when the conglomerated heap was disturbed by another drove passing across or into or out of the market. Great cruelty was practised, the poor animals being goaded on the flanks and struck on the head before they could be marshalled in their proper places. When one of them was sold a further scene of turmoil and ill-usage presented itself, for the poor animal was likely to run into other rings in the attempt to cross a crowded market and had to undergo another ordeal of goading and beating."

As early as 1766 a certain Mr. Glynn had advocated the removal of the cattle market from Smithfield and condemned the "intolerable practice of holding a market for the sale of live cattle in the centre of the metropolis". He suggested instead that Smithfield should become, "a noble regular square, which might be applied either for the purpose of trade, or else as dwellings for merchants and people of opulence, as should be found most convenient."

Public indignation at the continuation of the live cattle market mounted. The fouling of the streets by animals on their way to and from the market and the danger to pedestrians were of particular concern. By the 1830s the newspapers were making a meal of every incident:

"On Monday two accidents occurred through the nuisance of

Pugin and Rowlandson's famous view of the cattle market. Every available space is crammed with a dense mass of animals, all to fill London's stomachs.
Finsbury Library

Smithfield Market. The first occurred in High Holborn, opposite Kingsgate Street; a gentleman was knocked down by a very powerful bull, and before he could recover himself he was severely trampled upon and gored by the infuriated beast. The second accident occurred in Long Lane, Smithfield. Henry Bennet, a lad of scarcely seven years of age, in attempting to cross the road was knocked down by a bullock proceeding from the market, and before he could be rescued wounds of a most shocking nature were inflicted.

"The same day a hog went into a house in Turnmill Street and very much mangled a young child, and 'tis judg'd would have eaten it, the nurse being asleep, had not a neighbour who heard it cry, run in to its relief."

Herds of cattle were also ambushed by gangs of thieves who would cosh the drovers and use the confusion of stampeding animals as cover for pickpocketing. Quite clearly Smithfield was no longer the ideal place for livestock or slaughterhouses. Charles Dickens added his pen to the growing antagonism against the market, and clearly sympathised with the campaigners of the day. In *Oliver Twist* there is a vivid description:

"It was market morning. The ground was covered, nearly ankle-deep with filth and mire; a thick steam, perpetually rising from the reeking bodies of the cattle, and mingling with the fog, which seemed to rest upon the chimney-tops, hung heavily above. All the pens in the centre of the large area, and as many temporary pens as could be crowded into the vacant space, were filled with sheep; tied up to posts by the gutter side were long lines of beasts and oxen, three or four deep. Countrymen, butchers, drovers, hawkers, boys, thieves, idlers, and vagabonds of every low grade, were mingled together in a mass; the whistling of drovers, the barking of dogs, the bellowing and plunging of oxen, the bleating of sheep, the grunting and squeaking of pigs, the cries of hawkers, the shouts, oaths, and quarrelling on all sides; the ringing of bells and roar of voices, that issued from every public-house; the crowding, pushing, driving, beating, whooping, and yelling; the hideous and discordant din that resounded from every corner of the market; and the unwashed, unshaven, squalid, and dirty figures constantly running to and fro, and bursting in and out of the throng; rendered it a stunning and bewildering scene, which quite confounded the senses."

(Chapter XXI)

The impressionable Pip in *Great Expectations* despised Smithfield, "the shameful place, being all asmear with filth and fat and blood and foam, seemed to stick to me!"

The City Corporation refused to do anything to improve matters. In 1849 a Royal Commission was set up and recommended the removal of the market, but out of self-interest the Corporation rejected their findings – hardly surprising since the market produced a net income of almost £10,000 a year in the 1840s.

In 1835 a private attempt was made to open a rival market. An Act of Parliament was approved despite fierce opposition from the Corporation, Smithfield butchers, salesmen, bankers and other vested interests. The anti-Smithfield press enjoyed the opportunity for gentle sarcasm, "The citizens will be deprived of the wholesome excitement occasioned by the sight of half-strangled oxen dying of thirst, the bellowing of bullocks, and yelling of drovers; the salubrious smells arising from the City cellar-hole slaughter-dens; and many other delights which the said citizens have hitherto enjoyed in full swing." Undaunted, the instigator, a Mr. John Perkins, went through with his plans. Fifteen acres of land were bought in Islington, between the Lower Road (now Essex Road) and the Regent's Canal. Water pipes were laid, pens for 40,000 sheep, 7,000 cattle and 1,000 pigs, nearly half a mile of slated sheds, abattoirs, offices and taverns were built. The new market opened in March, 1836, but after a struggling existence of seven months the market died. Mr. Perkins lost £100,000, and within a few years the land was covered by a mass of terraced houses. Clearly rivalry was no solution; Smithfield itself must first be closed.

At last in 1852 the Commissioners won the day and the Smithfield Market Removal Act was passed, relocating the livestock market on a new open site north of Islington, called Copenhagen Fields. Copenhagen House and its surrounding meadows had long been famous as a tavern, tea-garden and cricket ground. In the eighteenth century Islington was renowned for its spas and resorts where well-to-do Londoners would venture on Sunday afternoons. By the mid-nineteenth century most of the old gardens were gone; Islington was no longer rural. The new livestock market was six times bigger than the old Smithfield market and could hold 50,000 animals with ease. Space, hygiene and efficiency were the essence of the design; no expense was spared. It was opened by Prince Albert on 13th June, 1855, and named the Caledonian Cattle Market; it had cost £350,000. The market and its associated pedlars' market flourished until 1939. History has now turned full circle; the clock tower and fine ornamental railings survive in a new recreation ground, although football is the order of the day rather than tea-gardens. Three of the four taverns which formed the corners of the market still stand.

On Monday 11th June, 1855, old Smithfield witnessed its last market. One might have thought that the market would have made a grand demonstration after 800 years' existence. Instead it was a small gathering and it died quietly. At 3 o'clock a few animals were still left unsold – some of Pharaoh's lean kine and long-legged, razor-backed sheep, almost transparently thin, pronounced by butchers alike as "rum uns". At 3.15 the great bell which stood in the middle of the market was rung for the last time and the market closed without ceremony.

A sentimental epitaph appeared in the *Illustrated London News*:

"Don't speak to me, Nat – I can't bear it! I'm fifty-four year old come tomorrow;

And of course in my time, in this walley of tears, I've had my 'lowance of sorrow.

I've burned three wives, but that's nothink – I mean nothink at all in comparasin –

To the high-pressure-burster-of biler-like feelings that now is my bosom a harrassin'.

To think that old Smithfield's done up! that the days of its glory is over!

As Miss Carrolwell sings at the consart, in her beautiful song, "The Disconsolate Drover".

Why doesn't I like the new market? Why, Nat, bless my heart, can you ask it?

Warn't I born here in Smithfield? – or, at least, what's as good, I was left in a basket.

Warn't the Happiest days of my life spent in John Street and Long Lane a goading

The bullocks as would lag behind, and make themselves so incommoding;

Or else hunting young pigs up the courts, which there is not a doubt had misled 'em;

Being much dirtier than the pigsties where their country sow-mothers had bred 'em;

Or twisting calves' tails to make 'em go straight, being a sort of boy at the weal a steering –

(Now I don't mean that for a joke, Mister Nat, so let's have none of your jeering);

Or else "prodding" the sheep which had come up to town for the first time that season,

And whose wits had gone woll-gatherin', though I don't know sheep is actuwated by reason,

'Cos they will run a-muck. Let 'em see a cart, cab or coal-waggon, and under they scrambles,

As though they wanted sudden death and a inques, and not a slaughterhouse and the shambles.

I knew how 'twould be when they was about to do away with the fair of old Bartlemee,

And I says to a medical stud (as stands early purl)

"Bartlemee's woted wulgar, so after that nothing'll startle me."

"Well," says he, "that's a blister; and was I a man in your highly

respectable station
I'd do what Wat Tyler did years ago here in Smiffield – pitch into
the Lord Mayor and Corporation.
"Why," says he, "they've done horrid things here afore – burn
heretics when con-trary!"
"Heretics," says I, "what was they?" "O," says he, "a breed that
went out with Queen Mary."
"But what was that to bursting up Bartlemy Fair? It's really past
bearin':
They'll move Smiffield Market next, and we shall lose the true
art of swearing."
And they've done it! The last market-day is tomorrow, and I can't
speak for exasperation.
But mark my words, Nat – we may take Sebastopol, but we've
lost Smiffield, and it's up with the British nation!
I'm a "down pin," Nat – Yes I am! When I croak will you go to the
Ram Inn and ask Mr. Farey,
If he'll let you nail up my badge in the tap-room, and find room for
me in his arey?
I think I might rest there, but if my ghost should walk it shall ask
his pardon.
But I've heard – *The Wedgetarians has bought Smiffield and
intend to conwert it into a Kitchen Garden."*

On Friday, 15th June, salesmen, bankers, butchers, drovers and
dogs transferred their allegiance to the new market.

The riotous Bartholomew Fair was also closed down in 1855. The
traditional rowdiness and confusion, which had incited mob unrest
and violence, were no longer tolerated by Victorian society. Londoners were thus deprived of one of their oldest public holidays. (Official
bank holidays were not introduced until 1871). So also the gingerbread men, hot-pie vendors, costermongers and Jewish orange sellers
– "handsome nut-brown, dark-haired daughters of Israel, jewelled,
ribboned and smiling" – were robbed of their annual bonanza.

While the loss of the old Smithfield market and Bartholomew Fair
justified some nostalgia, the Shambles meat market at Newgate was
a disgrace. Animals from the cattle market were driven to be killed
and flayed in one of a hundred or so slaughterhouses nearby, most of
which were in basement or cellar premises. Conditions were confined, dark and filthy, while the Shambles market, the largest meat
market in the country, was hopelessly congested and inefficient:

"Through the filthy lanes and alleys no one could pass without
being butted with the dripping end of a quarter of beef, or
smeared by the greasy carcase of a newly-slain sheep. In many of
the narrow lanes there was hardly room for two persons to pass
abreast." *(Oliver Twist)*

Once again the Corporation was landlord, charging rents for stalls

and levying tolls on meat sold, but showing remarkably little concern for the miserable conditions or vile effluvia. Licensing controls on slaughterhouses were eventually introduced in 1848.

Within ten years the gap left by the livestock market and fair was filled by a new market for meat, equipped with all the latest facilities. This is the market that still functions today. The old Shambles were swept away and all the slaughtering moved up to Copenhagen Fields. The remaining space at Smithfield was laid out as a small public garden, surrounded by an impressive spiral ramp or rotunda leading down to the underground area. The building of the new Central Market was precipitated by a revolution in transport, for as the live cattle departed, the railway arrived.

Railways revolutionised the meat business. Before the advent of railways any livestock killed in the country was either eaten locally or preserved as salt-beef, hams and bacon for transport to the cities. Fresh meat could only be transported any distance on the hoof. As we have seen, this was time-consuming and wasteful. It was reckoned that cattle lost 20lb per animal on a 100-mile walk. Even before the closure of the old Smithfield market, railways were beginning to make a significant impact. In 1849 over half the two million animals sold at Smithfield came to London by rail. By 1854 this had reached two-thirds. Livestock arrived quicker and in much better condition. The speed and reliability of railways soon opened up new possibilities. By 1853, 40,000 tons of fresh meat was arriving in London by rail. This trend was irreversible; if old Smithfield cattle market had not been closed statutorily by Parliament, the railways would have seen to it within another decade.

Fantastic new feats of engineering were accomplished in building

60   *The rotunda, connecting street level*
      with the underground sidings under
      the new meat market. The gentle
      gradient was built for horses pulling
      carts. **Theo Bergström**

the railways – the colossal viaduct on the early London-Greenwich railway surpassed even the Roman aqueducts which had been unrivalled for 2,000 years. The original idea had been to have one enormous central terminus for London at Charing Cross, but this came to nothing as separate railway companies built individual stations at Paddington, Euston, Victoria, King's Cross, etc. In 1846 a terminus was proposed at Farringdon Street, to provide the Great Western, North Western and Great Northern railways with an extension to the City. The line was to run in a covered cutting from Paddington to King's Cross, and then south along the Fleet valley, in the process eliminating the ancient rookeries. Work began in 1859, funded jointly by Great Western and the City Corporation.

The engineer was Sir John Fowler, who built the Forth Bridge, and the task required all his brilliance. Excavations in the Fleet valley were extremely difficult and in 1862 there was a near disaster when the culvert holding the Fleet River burst and flooded all the workings up to King's Cross. Since then, however, the massive brick retaining walls, with the tangle of tunnels and subterranean bridges, have held firm.

The Metropolitan Line, as it was called, was opened in January 1863, the world's first underground railway. The original terminus station is in fact the large derelict building, black with soot and grime, on the corner of Farringdon Road and Cowcross Street.* The line was an instant success, carrying twelve million passengers in 1864. Trains ran every ten minutes, and the third-class fare was only 3d. Even so, the smoke from the steam engines must have been nightmarish, even with special smoke reducers, and would not have pleased today's anti-smoke lobby. In 1865 the line was extended to Moorgate, and the following year the Chatham and Dover line was brought over the river at Blackfriars to link up with Farringdon Street thus connecting the north and the south.

The railways demanded comparable improvements to the roads. Farringdon Road and Farringdon Street (originally Victoria Street, but soon renamed) were built in 1856 and the Fleet Market removed. Charterhouse Street, joining Holborn and Charterhouse Square, was formed beside the new market. In 1879 Clerkenwell Road was ruthlessly driven through the middle of St. John's Square to link Old Street with Theobald's Road and New Oxford Street. Before 1879 a quiet narrow lane, known as Wilderness Row, had run along the north side of the Charterhouse between St. John Street and Goswell Road. There was a grassy bank and ditch beside the Charterhouse wall and houses on the other side. Other lanes, such as Liquorpond Street, were also swallowed up; the Victorians had complete confidence in their abilities and were rarely conservation-minded.

Trams ran along Farringdon Road, Goswell Road and Clerkenwell Road by the 1890s:

* Demolished 1989, to make way for an
uninspiring office block.

61

"These primitive trams were cumbersome passenger vehicles; horse-drawn, they were slow, and were reversible by changing the horses from front to back for the return journey. Tram drivers put on the brake by turning a handle, and blew his horn whistle to warn a vehicle in front to get off the line, Fare 2d. all the way!"

The greatest achievement, however, was the Holborn Viaduct, linking Holborn with a straight wide road to Newgate Street. The plans, first mooted in *The Builder* in the 1840s, were implemented in 1863 to the design of William Heywood, surveyor to the City Corporation, and at a cost of £2½ million. Four hundred yards long, the viaduct spanned the Fleet valley on a series of bridges, the longest of which crosses Farringdon Road. The ornate cast-iron parapet, with four statues representing Commerce, Agriculture, Science and Fine Arts, is supported on massive granite piers, and offers a good view down Farringdon Street to Blackfriars. The speed and industry of the Victorian navvies, using only primitive tools and muscle power, was such that the viaduct was opened by Queen Victoria on 6th November, 1869.

The viaduct was flanked with grand new Italianate buildings including the City Temple Free Church, with its two-storeyed palladian portico, and Holborn Viaduct station. Only the facade of the City Temple survives from 1874; the rest was gutted in the war and rebuilt

*The bursting of the Fleet River and the destruction of the Metropolitan Railway – **Illustrated London News** This disaster did not deter the engineers.* **Guildhall Library**

in 1955. Underneath the bridge, connected by steps, is the original Oddbins wine cellar. The construction of Holborn Viaduct took part of St. Andrew's churchyard, and made 4,000 people homeless – there was no obligation to rehouse them in those days. At last, however, the notorious slums of the Fleet valley had been cleared away. Newspapers of the day filled their inside pages with a mixture of civic pride at the new improvements, and melodramatic accounts of the wickedness and crimes that had supposedly occurred in the alleys of Chick Lane and Field Lane. The demolition of the infamous Red Lion Inn, Three Cripples Tavern and Fagin's Kitchen in the 1840s was accompanied by a morbid sentimentality in the press.

The City Corporation's apathy in moving the cattle market was matched only by their indifference to conditions in Newgate prison. Convicted and unconvicted still shared the neglected cells and the licence and corruption of the previous century was replaced only by the harsh severity of Victorian justice. Dickens paints a grim picture of the place: "those dreadful walls of Newgate, which have hidden so much misery and such unspeakable anguish . . ." Pip "beat the prison dust off his feet, exhaled its air from his lungs, so contaminated did he feel." (*Great Expectations*)

Public executions continued to be much awaited events:

"The space before the prison was cleared, and a few strong

Farringdon railway cutting today, justifying the Victorians' unwavering confidence in their engineering ability. British Rail are now electrifying the lower line. **Theo Bergström**

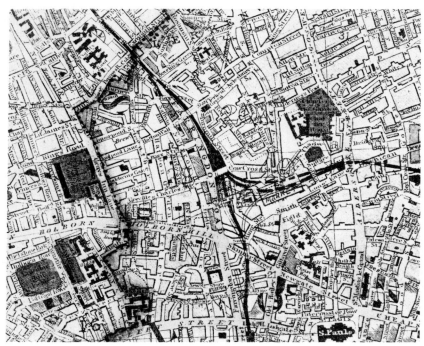

barriers, painted black, had been thrown across the road to break the pressure of the expected crowd, when Mr. Brownlow and Oliver appeared at the wicket, and presented an order of admission to the prisoner . . .

"A great multitude had already assembled; the windows were filled with people, smoking and playing cards to beguile the time; the crowds were pushing, quarrelling, joking. Everything told of life, and animation, but one dark cluster of objects in the centre of all – the black stage, the cross-beam, the rope, and all the hideous apparatus of death."   (*Oliver Twist*)

On 26th May, 1868, Michael Barret was hanged outside the main gate of the prison for his part in the Fenian outrage, a plot which involved blowing up part of the Clerkenwell House of Correction, which survived to become the Hugh Myddleton School. With the crowd yelling "hats off", this was the last public execution in England. Thereafter hangings took place in the execution shed, a tall timber lean-to within the prison compound.

In 1855 the Giltspur Street compter was demolished together with other smaller penal establishments like the Fleet prison, and prisoners were transferred to new model gaols such as Holloway and Pentonville. Newgate, the last bastion of medieval punishment, was itself torn down in 1902, and replaced with the impressive new Central Criminal Court, the Old Bailey. Mountford's design is one of the finest pieces of neo-English Baroque – an elegantly curved facade

*Cassell's **Immense Map of London**, 1866, shows the Victorian improvements in mid-stream. Holborn Viaduct and Clerkenwell Road are still on the drawing board.*   **Museum of London**

*Holborn Viaduct, spanning
Farringdon Road, adorned by the City
crest.* **Theo Bergström**

65

of Portland stone, and a dome surmounted by a twelve-feet-high figure of Justice, with her sword and scales. The dome is an important landmark, though rather overshadowed by St. Paul's.

In 1824 the General Post Office established its headquarters in St. Martin's-le-Grand. A magnificent building by Sir Robert Smirke was finished in 1829 (but regrettably demolished in 1910). Its grand Greek-style portico was very like the facade of the British Museum which Smirke had built in 1823. Trollope, the novelist, worked here between 1834 and 1841.

On the opposite side of the street, just south of St. Botolph's were a French Protestant church and the Bull and Mouth Inn, one of the famous coaching inns of its day. The Bull and Mouth, which was a strange corruption of 'Boulogne Mouth', had a courtyard and galleries rather like the George at Southwark which has happily been preserved. This and the many other inns in Aldersgate Street and Goswell Road thrived on the passenger and mail coaches which left St. Martin's for all parts of the country. The 1830s were the heyday of the stage coach; twenty-one coaches left for the north of England each day. The departure of the night mail must have been a thrilling event. The railways killed the coaches, and ruined the inns. In 1866 a pneumatic underground railway was dug from Euston to the Post Office, to speed the delivery of mail by avoiding the congested streets, and is still used today.

The Post Office grew, boosted by the uniform penny post, proposed by Rowland Hill in 1836 and adopted in 1840. In 1887 it expanded across the road, destroying the Bull and Mouth Inn, whose fine carved wooden sign now hangs nearby in the Museum of London. On

Public executions outside Newgate attracted large excitable crowds. Residents opposite made a tidy income by charging for a grandstand view.
Museum of London

Twin peaks of justice. This view of the
Old Bailey from Farringdon Street is
rapidly being obscured by steel and
glass. **Theo Bergström**

68   *The General Post Office,*
St. Martin's-le-Grand, in 1895. Note
the early open-topped omnibus in the
foreground. **G.L.C.**

the roof of the vast new grey building Guglielmo Marconi made the first public transmission of wireless signals on 27th July, 1896. Christ's Hospital School moved out to Horsham, Sussex, in 1902 and the Post Office took the site, building yet another monolithic block between St. Bartholomew's Hospital and Newgate Street, fronting onto King Edward Street. This houses the National Postal Museum, with its outstanding collection of nineteenth-century and commemorative British stamps – a philatelists' mecca. Outside stands Onslow Ford's fine statue of Rowland Hill.

The old graveyard behind St. Botolph's was laid out as a public garden with neat flower beds, chestnuts, limes, planes and fig trees, known aptly as Postman's Park. The tranquillity is ruffled only by Michael Ayrton's rather aggressive minotaur sculpture. On one side a small verandah contains fifty poignant plaques to heroic Victorian deeds:

> "Thomas Simpson died of exhaustion after saving many lives from the breaking ice at Highgate Ponds: 25th January, 1885"
> "Walter Peart, driver, and Harry Dean, fireman, of the Windsor Express on 18th July, 1898, whilst being scalded and burnt sacrificed their lives in saving the train."

By the nineteenth century Smithfield's smarter residential streets, such as Britton Street or Charterhouse Square, were no longer the height of fashion. Industry and commerce began to occupy many of the houses. Printing, publishing, clothing and meat processing all flourished in Smithfield; so did the precision and precious metal craft

70 *The demolition of Robert Smirke's magnificent facade. The replacement Post Office buildings are depressingly dull by comparison. Thank goodness his British Museum survives!* **Museum of London**

The galleried courtyard of the Bull
and Month Inn, a product of the
coaching age, painted by George
Shepperd in 1817. **Guildhall Library**

71

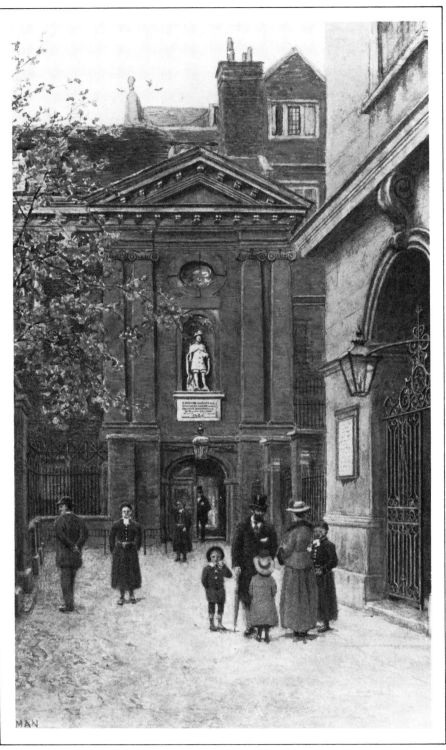

72 *Children and parents outside the*
    entrance to Christ's Hospital School.
    The tower of Wren's Christchurch is on
    the right. **Museum of London**

industries, centred on Clerkenwell and Hatton Garden – watches and clocks, scientific instruments, jewellery, gilding and plating; also Booth's Gin distillery, a more acceptable hang-over from Gin Lane!

New commercial buildings were erected to accommodate the growing activity at the heart of the Empire. Their large bulk was frequently made less oppressive by careful architectural details – decorated tiles, glass and ironwork, with coloured bricks or stone dressing – expensive, but sadly missing in modern, commercial architecture. Styles were very derivative; the gothic gable of Nos. 3–5 St. John Street with its mock-Tudor brick chimneys and elaborate date panel, the Italian renaissance 'palazzos' of Nos. 14–16 Cowcross Street or Nos. 34–36 St. John Street, the Dutch gables and terracotta of No. 30 St. John's Lane or No. 57 St. John Street, the Venetian gothic of Nos. 9–13 Cowcross Street.

Commercial offices – insurance, shipping brokers, solicitors, accountants, banks – accompanied the boom. Waterhouse's pompous gothic red-brick Prudential Assurance building in Holborn (1879) is a true monument to Victorian grandeur. Far more domestic are the attractive terraces fronting the north side of Snow Hill, including the fine bow-fronted police station. The old Saracen's Head Inn, where John Rough was caught, was demolished in the process; Saracen's

The quality of Victorian architecture contrasts sharply with the bland 1960s block behind. To the left a glimpse of The Charterhouse.
Theo Bergström

Building is the sole reminder of the site of this inn. Following the introduction of incandescent filament lamps in 1881, one of the first electricity generating stations was built on Holborn Viaduct, supplying nearby offices and the hospital.

The Victorian commercial buildings usually replaced smaller Georgian or earlier houses; redevelopment was preferred to rehabilitation or extensions. No doubt much of what they destroyed we would now preserve. The arched entrance to Cloth Fair and the row of pre-Fire gabled houses next to the church, similar to Nos. 41 and 42, were pulled down in 1905, despite protests from antiquarians. On the other hand, the concentration of commercial Victorian architecture in Smithfield, particularly St. John Street and Cowcross Street, is itself now rare in London.

By 1870 Smithfield's street pattern was complete, and remains almost unaltered today. Unlike much of the surrounding area, Smithfield was not flattened during or after the war. The Victorian improvements on what was basically its medieval layout had changed Smithfield "from one of the meanest to one of the handsomest parts of London" (*The Mirror*, 1874). It still has that potential, if the barbarians can be kept at bay.

74　*The Italian Renaissance style dominates Farmiloe's building at No. 34 St. John Street.* **Theo Bergström**

*Nos. 6-10 Cloth Fair, 1905. Passers-by
pose respectfully for the camera.
Conservationists failed to save these
17th-century houses from demolition.*
G.L.C.

76   *Smithfield's 'nave and screen' – cast
iron at its most elegant.*
Theo Bergström

CHAPTER·2·
THE MEAT MARKET

THE BUILDINGS

Smithfield, or to give it its correct name, The London Central Markets, is the largest wholesale meat market in the country, and the grandiose scale of the buildings clearly matches this function.

It occupies a very extensive site, almost ten acres, of which six and a half are covered by buildings and the rest by access roads. The market is long and narrow, stretching about 400 yards from Farringdon Road to Lindsey Street. Charterhouse Street runs along the north side and Long Lane and West Smithfield along the south side. There are three distinct parts to the Central Markets today; the meat market, the poultry market, and the general market. The meat section was there first, and the original buildings survive.

The principal factor influencing the plans for the meat market was the Metropolitan railway, which had been extended from Farringdon Street to Moorgate in 1865, and linked to the Southern Region in 1866. With the railway already underground, it was an obvious step to design the market on two levels – a basement for unloading meat from the railway, and the main market at ground level, easily accessible for the buyers' carts taking the meat away; a perfect concept at the time.

The removal of the live cattle market to Copenhagen Fields in 1855 had been a great success, but although London butchers continued to buy livestock there and slaughter it themselves, more and more meat was arriving direct by rail, already slaughtered. This was due largely to the cheapness and speed of rail travel, which obviated the long exhausting droves for the animals and also kept the meat fresh, but was also a result of new restrictions placed on the movement of live animals to prevent the spread of livestock diseases from infected areas. New slaughterhouses were set up in the provinces and although the Caledonian Cattle Market continued, the great days of the drover were numbered. With the completion of the Metropolitan Railway, Smithfield was linked by rail to all parts of the United Kingdom.

In 1860 the City Corporation obtained an Act of Parliament for erecting new market buildings at Smithfield and another in 1861 for doing away with the old Shambles meat market at Newgate. £235,000 was raised to purchase the necessary extra land (this included the burial ground of St. Sepulchre's church) and £200,000 for construction.

Sir Horace Jones, the City Architect, was appointed to design the new market. This was to be his first major success and opened the way for his later commissions for Billingsgate Market (1875) and Leadenhall Market (1881). His magnum opus, which will surely outlast all the others, if only crossing an American lake, was Tower Bridge, designed jointly with Wolfe Barry, the engineer.

Work on the new Smithfield market began in 1866. Tremendous excavations were necessary for the basement area, with large sidings for unloading the meat trains. Thousands of navvies were hired to loosen and remove 172,000 tons of earth. Twenty enormous main girders, each 240 feet long, were carried across the width of the hole, supported on 180 gigantic wrought-iron stanchions. Cross-girders were then laid and the gaps filled with brick arching, all to support the stone floor of the market above. Altogether five miles of iron girders were used. In the basement powerful hydraulic lifts were installed to raise the meat from the railway sidings into the market (see front cover). On top of this colossal platform the market building was erected, the first stone laid in June, 1867, and completed a year

78 *Smithfield market, 1870. Substitute lorries for horses, diesel fumes for manure and you have 1980. The statues guarding the Grand Avenue witness every change.* **Finsbury Library**

later. It is a masterpiece of functional and aesthetic design – 630 feet long and 246 feet wide.

The style is vaguely Italianate, but more noticeably shows the influence of Paxton's Crystal Palace whose glass and iron extravaganza, built for the Great Exhibition of 1851 in Kensington Gardens, was the marvel of London. The outside walls are a series of arcaded recesses, Portland stone Doric pilasters supporting round arches with richly carved keystones. The recesses are filled with red brickwork and fancy grillwork, elegantly coiled and twisted. At the four corners are octagonal pavilion towers, each with a dome and sporting grotesquely carved stone griffins flaunting the City coat-of-arms. The length of the building is relieved by a central arcade, the Grand Avenue, which divides the market in two. The entrances are impressive; huge statues, representing London, Edinburgh, Dublin and Liverpool stand guard at each end and fiery bronze dragons glare down at the paving. Roofed by an elliptical iron arch, the Grand Avenue is shut off from the interior of the market by open ironwork screens, fourteen feet high, which carry ranks of old decorative gas lamps mounted on brackets. Access into the market is through two sets of intricate iron gates each twenty-five feet high, nineteen feet wide and weighing fifteen tons. The hinges are prodigious.

Inside the market, a central avenue provides a splendid view of the entire length of the building. The lofty round-arched roof, supported on tall columns with side arches, is like a cathedral nave. The elaborate cast-iron, smartly painted in bright azure blue, is as skilfully used here as in any of the great London railway stations. Either side of the main thoroughfare are the sellers' stalls, 162 altogether, each about thirty-six feet long by fifteen feet wide with overhead rails festooned with meat hooks. Small areas have now been partitioned off as offices or refrigerators, but the atmosphere is still one of great space and airiness.

The use of open ironwork was Sir Horace Jones's masterstroke – letting in the light and air while the louvred roof keeps out the sun. In summer, temperatures are substantially lower in the market than in the shade outside, which is excellent for keeping meat fresh. The ventilation of hanging meat is said by discerning carnivores to be one of Smithfield's assets which pre-packed supermarket meat lacks.

The opening ceremony on 24th November, 1868, was an extravagant affair. Headed by the Lord Mayor, 1,200 guests sat down in the new building to 'dejeuner at two o'clock', a banquet of boars' heads and barons of beef amid a festive atmosphere – gas-lit candelabras, music from the Grenadier Guards, and back-slapping speeches by all the notables present. The toast was "tolls to the Corporation, cheap meat to the people and fair profits to the salesmen". And so it proved; the market was an instant success. The rents and tolls quickly repaid the Corporation's capital outlay for construction, competition for the

80   *Iron dragons and lions on Holborn*
        Viaduct survey the market buildings
        below. **Theo Bergström**

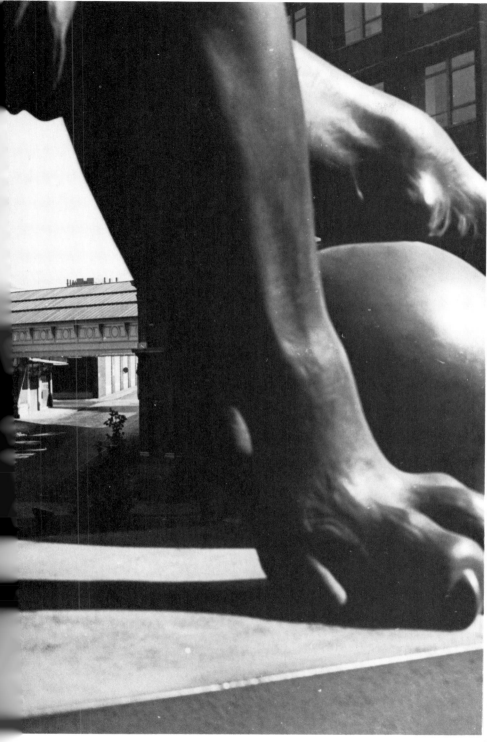

82   *Smithfield's distinctive towers – the
north side of the market along
Charterhouse Street. The canopy
keeps the rain off, but ruins the facade.*
Theo Bergström

market stalls was vigorous, and the populace got their meat fresh.

In 1873 the market was extended by a new poultry market erected immediately west of the meat market. Two further buildings, both unpretentiously designed, were added in 1879 and 1899 west of the poultry market fronting onto Farringdon Road and Snow Hill called the General Market. These were originally intended for fruit, flowers, vegetables and fish, and to accommodate the old Fleet and Farringdon Street market. This had handled rather ordinary produce, "the plebeian cabbage, the modest onion, the homely apple, and the barely respectable cauliflower". It was the pitch of Mayhew's celebrated watercress sellers. Up to a ton of watercress was carried up to town each week by the Great Western Railway from Cookham and Rickmansworth. The old street market had been a poor affair, "a melancholy intermingling of closed shops and stalls". The General Market fared no better. Covent Garden rapidly pinched its trade, and fish could not compete with Billingsgate. For many years now the General Market has been used by the meat and poultry trade.

In the early 1880s the first imports of frozen meat from Australia, New Zealand and South America, arrived in London's docks. Enormous cold stores were needed to hold the meat before it was sold in the market. Two of the biggest were built in Charterhouse Street opposite the poultry and general markets. Both are now empty, the Port of London Authority's store* and the Corporation's 'White House', huge relics of imperial trading.

The market buildings were only slightly damaged in the war,† but in 1958 a serious fire destroyed the poultry market, leaving a gap between the meat and general markets. The fire broke out underground in the early hours and became a raging inferno before the traders above realised anything was amiss. The evacuation of people and merchandise was successful, but too late to prevent the total destruction of the building. The new poultry market, designed by Sir Thomas Bennett, was completed in 1962–3, costing £2,000,000. The huge reinforced concrete grey brick and glass structure, which in 1963 had the largest clear spanning dome roof (225 feet) in Europe, is rather like an Olympic swimming pool in appearance. Automatic ventilation, covered unloading bays, office accommodation and a new pub for the market were incorporated, and perhaps explain the comparative efficiency of the poultry market today.

In 1965 part of the general market was converted to provide storage for hand trucks and changing facilities for workers, but the biggest improvement came in 1970. With no more meat deliveries by rail after the early 1960s, the vast underground area was converted into a cavernous car park, removing the sidings and lifts. Passenger trains now rumble through to Moorgate on the far side of a screen wall. More recently, a plastic canopy has been fixed round the outside of the meat market buildings to provide shelter for loading. Func-

---

*Burnt out in 1989.
†A V2 rocket landed near Hart's
Corner in Farringdon Street in 1945.

tional, but not very pretty, it hardly adds to the skilful detailing of Horace Jones's building.

HOW THE MARKET WORKS

Smithfield Market is owned and run by the Corporation of London in its capacity as a private owner of land rather than as a local authority. The Corporation is unique in having this dual function and results from its having a corporate identity long before local government existed elsewhere other than round the parish pump. Under the management of the Market Superintendent and his staff, the Corporation maintain and repair the buildings, clean the streets and pavings, remove refuse, keep law and order with their special police force, and supply over seven million units of electricity each year. There is also the duty of hygiene control, and the meat inspectors ensure that no bad meat enters or is sold in the market. Official meat inspectors were paid to catch rogue dealers in the old Shambles meat market. In medieval times anyone found selling putrid meat would have been stuck in the pillory with the offending meat burning under his nose, while in Victorian times condemned meat was taken to the boiling house, and the perpetrator flogged. Today there is no pillory, but the discovery of a diseased carcase will usually mean that the whole batch or lorryload must be destroyed.

To pay for these services, rents are collected from the tenants of the market stalls and a toll is levied on the weight of meat sold, just like it was in the old Shambles market. The market is expected to pay for itself – it cannot be subsidised like a public swimming bath, for example. The amount of profit made depends on the cost of providing the services balanced against how much rent and toll the Corporation think they can reasonably charge without driving the tenants away.

There are about seventy tenants in the market, between them renting the 230 stalls. Until 1978 all the tenancies were still on a weekly basis, with no security of tenure or guarantees of rent levels, not that this has prevented some firms holding tenancies since the market opened in 1868. After prolonged negotiations, twelve-year leases have now been granted by the Corporation with the tenants sharing some of the responsibilities for maintenance costs. This should help tenants to borrow and invest capital.

Tenants range from small local businesses to the largest national meat wholesaling firms. Borthwick's, for example, who started life when Thomas Borthwick took a stall in 1892, are now one of the biggest public companies in the country, owning Matthews, the high street butchers. Largest of all, however, are the Vestey Group, which still operates as a private company. Vestey's were pioneers of integration, being involved in all aspects of the meat trade. The group contains British Beef Co., second largest fresh meat slaughterers in the United Kingdom, Blue Star Line who carry meat from all over the world, Union Cold Storage, Weddel, one of the biggest wholesale distributors and a major stall-holder at Smithfield, and, perhaps best known, Dewhurst, the high street butcher, with over 1,500 retail shops throughout Britain. Despite their scale of operation, Smithfield is still their headquarters.

Although some stalls in the market attract more business, rents are uniform regardless of position. Martinelli's, who have expanded rapidly in recent years, rent the coveted spot beside the Grand Avenue, known as 'Peter's under the clock'.

The market operates five times a week, Monday to Friday, at night. This has advantages; the central London streets are quiet and market traffic does not choke the area as it would during the day; at night it is cooler, which keeps the meat fresher; and by buying his meat early in the morning, the butcher can have fresh meat in his shop when the shopping day starts.

Unlike many wholesale markets, such as Covent Garden or Billingsgate, Smithfield is not a sample market. Everything for sale has to be unloaded, carried into the market, displayed, purchased and carried out again. At Covent Garden lorries often act as mobile warehouses – a buyer will examine one box of oranges and buy the whole lorryload. More sensible and quicker, one might think, but Smithfield is unique, and traditional.

Unloading starts at midnight when the market gates open. Large lorries will have been arriving throughout the afternoon and evening from all over the British Isles and Europe. The origin of meat at Smithfield has changed considerably during the last thirty years. Before the war 80% was imported through the docks, mainly from Argentina and the old Commonwealth countries. 330,000 tons of imported meat were sold at Smithfield in 1938, but by 1968 this had dwindled to 150,000 tons, and by 1975 to 50,000 tons, less than one-quarter of the total meat sold. Foot and mouth disease in 1967 virtually put paid to Argentinian imports, while the European Economic Community has increasingly squeezed out old Commonwealth produce. Most meat now comes from the British Isles – Scottish and Irish beef, Welsh lamb, and West Country pigs; since joining the E.E.C. a lot of meat imports are continental, or from rather unexpected sources such as Botswana.

The reduction in numbers of lorries delivering in recent years has been compensated by their size; huge forty-feet long juggernauts are now the norm. If they arrive early, as continental lorries are liable to do, they lie up in St. John Street, their rumbling refrigeration engines annoying the neighbours. Manoeuvring these monsters into the unloading bays requires immense skill. With limited road widths

Unloading starts at midnight.

Pitching onto barrows.

2.50 a.m.

Lambs from the slaughter.

Sides of beef can weigh 400 lb.

The 'Smithfield shuffle'.

This little piggy went to market.

Paradise for the carnivore.

Cutting, a highly skilled job.

Shopmen weigh and mark every carcase.

Many tenants have their own cold stores.

4.30 a.m. A rest before trading begins.
Theo Bergström

it is hard to believe that the lorries could be any longer. The damage done to pavements, kerbs and bollards suggests they are already too big.

The labour force at Smithfield totals about 2,700,* and is split into many clearly demarcated jobs, between which there is little interchange. Meat arriving by lorry is handled first by 'pullers-back' whose job is to pull the meat back to the tailboard of the vehicle, where it is carried by 'pitchers' into the market. The carcases are pitched onto the rows of hooks hanging in the stalls.

Pitchers work in gangs, either employed directly by a market tenant with regular deliveries, or self-employed. Most of the 800–900 tons of meat (on average) sold each night is still carried by hand, exactly as it was a century ago. This is hard physical work. Each carcase is lowered onto the shoulders of a pitcher who half runs, half walks to the stall, trying to minimise the time the weight is on his back. This is known as the 'Smithfield shuffle', one arm swinging free, eyes fixed doggedly ahead, blasphemy to anyone in the way! Long sides of beef, which might weigh 400 lbs (approx. 180 kg) are carried by two pitchers, synchronised like clockwork. Work on piece-rate is no job for the faint of heart and must hasten many a hernia.

In the poultry market pitching is less arduous and less spectacular – most chickens arrive pre-packed in cartons which are handled easily by trucks and rollers. There are always a few turkeys hanging up, lots at Christmas of course, and rabbits, hares and pheasants in season. However, the great variety of poultry once available is gone; French geese, ptarmigan, quail, pigeon and partridge in Victorian times; swans, herons, curlews and thrushes in Chaucer's day. Plovers' eggs were once a Smithfield delicacy, and the first of the season was always a gift to Queen Victoria.

By 4.00 a.m. the large lorries have dispersed and the market is almost full; a fine sight, with row upon row of pigs, lambs, ewes, bullocks and calves hanging from their hooks. Inside the market a large number of men, known as 'shopmen', work at the stalls, weighing and checking in the meat, humping carcases around the stall for display, and cutting them into different portions. Much of the meat still comes in carcase form, and dividing the animal into primary joints is a highly skilled job. Indeed 80% of the carcases are cut up within the market into manageable joints for the retail butcher. Whole pigs are strung between two lines of hooks and a few expertly aimed hacks with an ugly sharp knife splits them in two. The piles of severed heads, their eyes staring hypnotically, go for brawn. Huge bins brimming with hearts, livers and entrails, or carefully folded strips of suet, await the offal merchant. This is the most coveted feature of Smithfield, where every part of the animal is sold to someone and nothing is wasted. Accidents during cutting are fortunately rare but nasty, and the proximity of St. Bartholomew's Hospi-

*Ten years on this is now less than 2,000.

tal is always reassuring. In recent years increasing amounts of meat are arriving already cut, boned and packed, as abattoirs have evolved from mere slaughterhouses into meat factories. This plainly saves much unnecessary transport, but if the trend continues in the long run it may be the undoing of Smithfield.

The gates open for trading at 5.00 a.m., wholesale only. Buyers vary as much as the market tenants, from large retail butchers to small cafe proprietors or hoteliers. The West End restaurant trade is said to be growing fast, perhaps because Smithfield is the only place where one can rely on finding large amounts of any cut of meat.

A great deal of home-produced meat is sold on a commission basis, where the market tenant does not own the meat but is a selling agent. He will try to get the highest price to increase his rake-off, while the buyer will seek the best for his money. All sales in the market are negotiated between buyer and seller, and no fixed prices are displayed. The bargaining system is one of Smithfield's main attractions. Prices fluctuate with supply and demand and may change during the course of a night's trading. However, once a price is agreed both buyer and seller abide by their word. The tradition of the merchants' integrity continues at Smithfield. At midday the Smithfield *Daily Report* publishes the closing prices of all the different cuts, and acts as a national barometer for meat prices.

In the meat market a buyer can only remove as much meat as he himself can carry in one journey; strangely this rule does not apply in the poultry market. Porters take the rest, either working directly for firms of carriers and large retail companies, or self-employed hired on a casual basis. These are the well-known 'bummarees'. All porters must have a licence, issued by the Market Superintendent, and there is a long waiting list. The bummarees, like the self-employed pitchers, charge per piece carried, and demand cash payment. They work fast and earn far more than those in regular employment. Bummarees are a fairly down-to-earth bunch; any stranger or cameraman is a suspected tax official or plain-clothes policeman. Perhaps it is just natural mistrust!

There is, however, tremendous camaraderie and loyalty among the men, many of whom have family ties with the market stretching back for generations. Indeed, it is difficult to become a market worker without some kinship connections; the absence of ethnic minorities other than among the street cleaners is a fair indication. Wage differentials between regular and self-employed workers has caused trouble and ill-feeling and even led to the occasional strike. Although the Transport and General Workers Union enjoys a 'closed shop' among all the manual workers, there is no effective central control and in a dispute sectional interests are defended obstinately. All suggestions for eliminating the self-employed sectors receive a frigid response.

By 8.00 a.m. most of the business is done. The meat is loaded onto dozens of retailers' vans and lorries for distribution in London and the Home Counties, or pulled by barrow to nearby premises for processing. It is rare for any fresh or 'bright' meat to remain unsold. By midday the market is usually clear, leaving the street cleaners to hose down the pavements and wash away the sickening stench of sagging flesh. The gutters run with blood and sawdust, while refuse lorries collect the metal skips piled with bones and cartons. Within a few hours, unless it is Friday and the weekend, the giant lorries will start to arrive for the following night's market.

SPIN-OFF TRADES*

The streets in the surrounding area are full of firms and businesses related in some way to the market and its produce. A few businesses originate from the days of the livestock market – a handful of leather and button dealers, and even a tennis racket gut firm who once would have obtained their raw materials direct from the Smithfield slaughterhouses. Far more numerous are the firms within a few hundred yards of the market which are engaged in the meat or poultry trades, actively related to the existing market. The 120 firms employ nearly 3,000 people and include modern administrative headquarters, such as Dewhurst House, but also offal merchants, sausage-skin makers, ham and bacon curers, pie makers, butchers' equipment shops and cold stores. In addition, there are thirty firms dealing in other food and drink, not related to the market.

There are many family businesses; Legrand's at the bottom of Cowcross Street has been handed down from father to son for three generations; close by, Donald Sproat, dealers in game for seventy years, still have a Sproat in charge. Many firms still buy at least some of their meat at the market. Dumenil's for example, who make hamburgers and portion chickens, get regular supplies from the market. Others may get direct deliveries and only top up from Smithfield. There are countless local links between firms, sharing part-load deliveries and keeping the butchers' equipment shops in business. Smithfield is *the* traditional and historically prestigious location.

Today much is changing. There are traffic problems; many Smithfield streets like Cowcross Street or St. John's Lane are very narrow and hopelessly unsuitable for those enormous container lorries which have to deliver supplies. Many buildings are old, unable to take machinery or expensive to modernise. Public health inspectors from the London Borough of Islington and the City Corporation, who control the area north and south of the market, wage a constant battle to encourage improvements in conditions. New E.E.C. hygiene

*Much has changed in the decade since 1980, and many of the activities and traders described below have now disappeared, as predicted.

regulations have brought stricter standards for food premises and some closures have been inevitable.

Sadly the traditional manufacturing and processing is dying, leaving only administrative functions. In 1951 there were thirty-one offal merchants and sausage makers in the area; by 1978 these had dwindled to only eleven. Most simply disappeared, either through lack of custom, or because there was no-one to take on the family business, or because they were forced to sell up when the lease expired. Some successful firms have moved to pastures new, in order to expand into modern premises with better access and more attractive conditions for their workers. Hensons, the last offal merchant to leave, moved to York Way, Holloway, apparently because so much was being stolen

The elliptical arch of the Grand Avenue. Traditional barrows and modern lorries below.
Theo Bergström

off the streets. In Smithfield things all too easily fall off the backs of lorries! Matthews, who left for Woolwich but returned to St. John's Lane a year later, are an exception to the trend.

In the next ten years many others will depart or close down. Some only survive now because the rents have been fixed for so long, or because they happen to own the freehold. Instead of turning up our noses at the bloodstained pavements or the thick smell of entrails or bacon smoke, or blocking our ears to the whine of saws grinding through cartilage and bone, perhaps we should savour the atmosphere before it is gone:

> "Here in Smithfield where my mother bought her weekly supplies was a spacious bacon curing and smoking business, whose real industry provided sides of the finest bacon turned out from their six large tall stacks, holding fifteen sides hanging in high rows over smouldering sawdust and burning slowly, logs all of a special kind of wood. I've seen the heavy doors open, and in boyish wonder thought where all this bacon went, as the bacon was lowered, sewn into rough covers of sacking and carted away." *(Finsbury resident 1956)*

The decline in cold stores has been even more dramatic. Ninety-nine per cent of their business is imported frozen meat from the docks, and the tremendous fall in these imports has ruined most cold stores. In the 1950s they employed over 500 men; now there are only 50. Union problems have scarcely helped (Smithfield is within five miles of the docks and therefore subject to the National Dock Labour Board rules). Most market tenants have installed their own small freezing units to be independent. A few cold stores may survive, such as Hedley Vicars in Cowcross Street, but for the others, huge purpose-built 'temples' for Argentinian beef and lamb, there can be no hope of revival. Nor is there much prospect of alternative use for these caverns, and no knowing what will happen when the frozen subsoil thaws.

Other activities in the area associated with the meat market include the Smithfield Department of Food Technology (formerly the Smithfield Meat College), now part of the Inner London Education Authority College for the Distributive Trades. This occupies the former school in Eagle Court and a modern block in Briset Street. Students come from all over the country and overseas. The college prepares students for the Institutes of Meat examinations and also runs courses in advanced food technology, meat manufacturing and meat inspection, as well as special courses for the Army Catering Corps.

At Nos. 87–88 Bartholomew Close is the Butchers' Hall, home of the Worshipful Company of Butchers, one of the City's oldest guilds, founded in 1364. Rebuilt in 1959 after war damage, it is far more lavish inside than out. Over the entrance are their coat-of-arms and motto: *Omnia subjecisti sub pedibus oves et boves* – that is, all sheep and cattle are under his feet.

The annual Smithfield Show, run by the Royal Smithfield Club, is a reminder of the past glories of the livestock market. Supreme champions of live cattle, sheep and pigs, are exhibited and auctioned, and prize carcases of pork, lamb, veal and beef are judged. At one time, weight alone was the prime attraction. Hence some Victorian criticism of the Show:

> "So far as respects the creatures themselves, they are certainly rather to be pitied than otherwise; for a pig so fat that he can neither see out of his eyes nor stand upon his legs, and who is furnished with a block of wood to support his snout for fear of suffocation among the straw of his litter, must have rather a burdensome life of it."

> "The Parisians in their cattle shows have given names of 'Oncle Tom', 'Bomarsund', and 'Sebastopol' to their prize animals; we have not yet risen to the dignity of thus naming our choice bullocks!"

Fortunately more than pure bulk is now taken into account. The Show used to be held at the Royal Agricultural Hall in Islington (built in 1862 by the Royal Smithfield Club and perhaps soon to be transformed from a decaying wreck into a Dickens Disneyland),* but moved to Earl's Court after the war.

THE MARKET'S FUTURE†

Smithfield is by far the largest meat market in the country, selling about 8% of total U.K. wholesale meat and poultry, and is the wholesale market for about eight million Londoners. In the region of 90,000 tons of beef and veal, 50,000 tons of mutton and lamb, 35,000 tons of pork, and 40,000 tons of poultry, were sold in 1977, representing well over £100 million. In Chaucer's day lambs sold for about 7d; a side of beef today is worth hundreds of pounds.

However, the amount of meat sold at Smithfield has fallen steadily over the last fifteen years. 1963 was something of a peak, with 400,000 tons (13% of the U.K. total). By 1968 it had dropped to 327,000 tons, and in 1975 to 233,000 tons. A 5% decline each year cannot be healthy; why is it happening?

As meat prices have risen in line with inflation, and with so many other things competing for the weekly pay packet, one might assume that we are eating less meat; in fact the housewife appears remarkably resilient and total U.K. consumption has not fallen significantly. Some of the fall in tonnage at Smithfield is due to de-boning and cutting at the abattoir – 100 tons of boneless meat could be the

---

*Finally saved and refurbished in 1985 as the Business Design Centre.
†This section summarizes the situation in 1980. See Chapter Eight for an updated résumé of the future prospects.

equivalent of 125 tons of carcase meat. However, the value of meat sold at Smithfield has also dropped in real terms, allowing for inflation; in 1976 it was only 77% of the 1969 value.

Before the war 80% of New Zealand mutton and lamb and 70% of Argentinian and New Zealand beef coming to this country passed through Smithfield market. It was without rival as a centre for the sale of surplus meat and poultry for the U.K., the Dominions, South America and Europe. Reductions in imported meat have severely affected Smithfield. In addition home-produced meat is increasingly being sold direct to retailers, by-passing Smithfield and other wholesale markets. Supermarkets have developed direct links with abattoirs, cutting out the middle men, and now some even operate slaughterhouses and processing factories of their own. All this cuts costs and brings competitive prices into the shops. In 1966 supermarkets and multiple chains sold only 9% of all retail meat, but by 1978 this was approaching 40%. The rest remains with family butchers and perhaps the fashion for 'small is beautiful' will keep them going and halt the trend. During the long, hot summers of 1976 and 1977 many shoppers were attracted by the cool hygienic packaged meat in supermarkets. The fierce price war since then has ensured that this custom has not been lost. Nevertheless, the prevalence and popularity of cellophane wrapping and packaging is surely a regrettable Americanisation of our society.

The increase in pre-packed meat at Smithfield – hundreds of boxes of silver-side, top-side, sirloin, etc. – will surely in time pave the way for a sample market. If this happens, how much of the enormous floorspace in the present buildings would be required? In the poultry trade 90% of supplies now go directly from the producers to the retailers. Only at peak times, like Christmas, do sizeable quantities pass through the market. Some stalls in the poultry and general markets do not bother to open every night, and a four-day week may be imminent. This is in spite of the fact that chicken and turkey consumption has increased enormously in recent years at the expense of other meats. Pre-packed, gutted, frozen or chilled, chicken is now a highly convenient food.

Within the market there are now fewer tenants; a result of less money to go round. Smaller men have been taken over by larger firms, an inevitable tendency nowadays. Although there is no apparent un-let space, some of the floor area once used for displaying and selling meat has been replaced by refrigerators or offices. The far end of the general market, known as the 'village', is now very quiet and almost deserted some nights.

The system of handling meat at Smithfield, with so many porters, pitchers and shopmen taking their cut, certainly does not encourage retailers to flock to the market. Some buyers prefer to get cheaper meat elsewhere and suburban wholesale meat depots, where delay and handling charges are less, have taken some of Smithfield's trade. Suburban meat depots were set up as a temporary measure during the war when Smithfield was closed, but several carried on when Smithfield re-opened in peacetime. Like Smithfield, they too have suffered from supermarket competition, or in some cases are in a poor location. However, they do attract Home Counties butchers who are not prepared to slog into Central London to Smithfield.

Whatever the pros and cons of the Smithfield set-up, for every £1.00 of Smithfield meat bought by the housewife 4p has been spent on labour at the market. Not surprisingly there are sages who claim that the unions are killing the market, by refusing to accept the rationalisation (and redundancy) which is essential if it is to survive. Admittedly, the numbers of men working in the market has fallen, but only in proportion to the reduced volume of meat handled. What is really needed in the long term is major reform and comprehensive mechanisation to cut down labour costs. At present a hard-working casual pitcher or bummaree can expect to earn £150 a week, cash. One forklift truck could probably do the work of ten bummarees or pitchers in the same time.

Forklift trucks are now used to good effect in the poultry market, where the boxes of chicken can easily be stacked onto pallets. It is not so easy in the meat market. The building is old and the congested gangways and stalls were not designed for large forklift trucks. However, at *Les Halles*, the old meat market in Paris which was built in 1858, special mini-forklift trucks with moveable arms were very successfully used for pitching and carrying out meat.

There are lots of possibilities – an overhead power-operated rail system with moving hooks could speed deliveries and reduce congestion; a central computer could assist accounting and book-keeping. But all this requires money, as well as the will to change. Up to now there has been a stubborn pride in the traditions of the market. The sturdy old wooden hand barrows with their steel-rimmed wheels which all the bummarees still use, have not changed for 100 years – plainly an excellent design, and quaint to look at, but hardly mechanisation. Although mechanical cutting of quarters and sides was introduced in the early 1900s, nearly all meat cutting is still done the old-fashioned way, by hand, whereas our European neighbours use power-saws and electric knives. Anachronistic methods are labour intensive and provide valuable employment for hundreds of men, but may also bring a slow death to the market – a common dilemma facing British industry.

Some 'experts' have suggested that the Smithfield buildings are too antiquated and badly situated to be worth even trying to improve, and that the sensible solution lies in moving the market to a new site. This has been done in Paris; *Les Halles* was closed in 1971 and moved to a new modern market in the suburbs at *La Villette*. The redevelopment of the old site for expensive hotels and offices would have paid for the scheme, although the French politicians are now thinking of making the space into a park.

In London the same has happened with Covent Garden vegetable market which was moved in 1974 to Nine Elms, south of the river, amid furious debate. Certainly the hopeless tangles of market-bound lorries and West End theatre traffic have been unravelled and the empty buildings are now being increasingly occupied by boutiques, beauty clinics, health food shops and trendy bistros for the bourgeois (not to mention sunken Chinese gardens), but the new market at Nine Elms has hardly been an economic success story. The government has already written off £19 million, and it is unlikely that they or the City Corporation would wish to repeat the exercise. Moreover, despite the colossal value of the Smithfield site on paper for city office redevelopment, two factors limit the real value; firstly, decking over the railway would be fantastically expensive and, secondly, the meat market buildings are listed by the Department of the Environment as being of special architectural and historic interest. Nor is traffic such a problem in Smithfield as was the case at Covent Garden. The decline in trade, the one-way system round the market, and the underground car park have virtually eliminated serious congestion. Many Smithfield market tenants remain highly suspicious, however, particularly of the Greater London Council who were behind the Covent Garden move.

If the market is to stay where it is, some minor improvements may be necessary even in the short term. Some of the standards of working do not meet the conditions laid down in the Offices, Shops and Premises Act of 1963. Laundry, first-aid and lorry washing facilities are all needed, and could be housed in part of the general market if trade continues to contract. It has been argued that rebuilding the poultry market in 1962 was a big mistake and a waste of £2 million. Instead, the site could have been used for lorry parking, leaving the original Central Markets building for the meat trade, and the 'village' for poultry. It is easy to argue this in retrospect, but the subsequent decline in trade was difficult to predict in 1960.

Hygiene standards in the market are adequate, endorsing the excellence of the original market design, but E.E.C. officials might wince at the sight of a carcase falling off a cart into the gutter, only to be promptly shoved back on the pile! What the eye doesn't see the heart doesn't bleed over. No-one knows yet whether new standards, requiring stainless steel floors for example, will be imposed by the 'Eurocrats'. Smithfield would find the cost hard to bear.

Suggestions for using the market buildings in other ways have so far fallen on stony ground. "Incompatible, impractical, unnecessary" is the immediate reply from the market tenants, although the occasional dance or 'meat ball' has always been a success. When trade

drops and rents rise they may think again. If the market contracts to a four-day week, why not start a general retail market on Saturday or Sunday morning? Petticoat Lane is chronically overcrowded and has little cover from the weather. Smithfield is central, parking is easy at weekends, and it is a magnificent building. Alternatively Billingsgate fish market, which is declining and threatened by a new road and a Colonel Seifert office block, could be moved into the old general market at the Farringdon Road end. Hygiene or traffic problems need not be insurmountable. Some forward-looking tenants have already branched out into the retail deep-freeze trade, with an eye to luring the lunchtime city office workers.

Alas, at present, no single authority is prepared to think very far ahead or invest any money. Recently the City Corporation and the London Borough of Islington Planning Authorities undertook a long-awaited joint study of the market and surrounding area (the local authority boundary runs just north of the market buildings). The recommendations for the market are innocuous and myopic, and the chance to examine thoroughly the long-term future of the market has been wasted.

All the evidence suggests that if recent trends continue without some change or flexibility occurring, Smithfield will die. The closure of the market would be a tragic loss to the Smithfield area and to all London. Thousands of men would lose their jobs, many of whom live fairly locally. Cafes would close and most of the spin-off trades would lose any remaining reason for staying in Smithfield. Meat has been Smithfield's trademark for hundreds of years; the next twenty years may sadly see the end of that tradition.

The end of a day's trading at
Smithfield. The seated statue still
looks on, but for how long?
Theo Bergström

98 *The traditional image of Bart's, caring for London's poor and sick. This little statue stands in the Great Hall of the Hospital.* **Theo Bergström**

CHAPTER·3·

ST. BARTHOLOMEW'S HOSPITAL

St. Bartholomew's Hospital rivals the meat and cattle market as the longest established and largest institution in the area. Like the meat market, it still occupies the site of its medieval foundation (it is the only London hospital with this distinction), although it too has expanded substantially outside its original precinct. The hospital covers a large part of the area south of the market. The old precinct is bordered by Giltspur Street, Little Britain and the Post Office to the south (this boundary used to be the city wall), but hospital buildings now spread east of Little Britain into Bartholomew Close. 'Bart's' is just as much part of Smithfield's character as the meat market; the white-coated doctors and hospital staff are as familiar in the streets as the barrows and blood-stained white coats of the meat workers.

The hospital was founded together with the Priory of St. Bartholomew's in 1123 by Rahere, described by Stow as "a pleasant witted gentleman". The story goes that in his youth he was a minstrel and fun-lover at the king's court, but in middle age he reformed his ways after catching malaria on a pilgrimage to Rome, vowing to set up a hospital and church to serve London's poor should he recover. On his return to health and to England he persuaded King Henry I to grant some land at Smithfield, just outside the city wall, where he duly fulfilled his side of the bargain.

The early hospital was run by the prior and monks who dispensed alms and gave what medical care they could. In the main, treatment was spiritual. In medieval times people feared for the salvation of their souls as much as for the health of their mortal bodies: many 'illnesses' were probably psychosomatic.

The hospital was expanded in Edward III's reign, and achieved some independence from the priory. Staffing consisted of a master, eight brethren and four sisters. Its own church was built, St.

Bartholomew-the-Less, which still stands today, just inside the main gate of the hospital. In 1423 Dick Whittington's will provided a handsome sum for the upkeep of the hospital. Physicians were usually theologians, scantily trained in traditional Greek, Roman or Arabic practices, but often resorting to quack herbal or astrological remedies. Only very simple operations were performed, and then at great peril to the unfortunate victim. One of the outstanding medieval medical treatises was written by John Mirfield at St. Bartholomew's, and his *Breviarum Bartholomei* became a universal text book of the day.

When the Priory of St. Bartholomew's was dissolved by Henry VIII in the Reformation, the hospital was valued at 35 pounds, 5 shillings and 7 pence, but being the largest in the city and fulfilling an immense social service it was not closed. One of Henry's last gestures was to refound the hospital under a royal charter, providing an income for 100 beds and a permanent staff of doctors and surgeons. Money was levied by a 'Poor Rate on Householders' within the city — the first of its kind in the country. This system of poor relief also financed Christ's Hospital School for deserted children. From then on civic charity no longer depended solely on the generosity of individuals, although personal gifts and endowments remain an important part of the hospital's income to this day.

Despite the improvements, accommodation was still totally inadequate. In the sixteenth century, St. Bartholomew's and St. Thomas's were the only London hospitals with beds for the sick, and as a result were hopelessly overcrowded. Medical knowledge was extremely sketchy and most deaths were attributed to 'convulsions'. Surgeons and physicians continued to be part-time or amateur, often distracted by other interests. Dr. Rodrigo Lopez, who was a hospital doctor for twenty years, was hanged for plotting to poison Elizabeth I. In 1665, the two senior physicians at St. Bartholomew's hastily abandoned their posts when the plague broke out.

There were changes for the better, however. New rules were laid down in the seventeenth century: "Every tenth bed is to be left empty to air and not more than one patient is to be put into each bed . . . no drink is to be brought in and sold to patients except by the physicians' and surgeons' licence." With an awakening spirit of scientific enquiry Bart's ceased to be just a refuge to care for the dying, but a place where serious efforts were made to cure the sick. Dr. William Harvey, who worked at Bart's from 1609 to 1643 discovered the circulation of blood. Anatomy lectures were given at the Royal College of Physicians near St. Paul's, using criminals' bodies for demonstrations. Before 1700, Bart's had no dissecting room of its own.

Although Bart's survived the Great Fire, saved by the city wall, the destruction of city property drastically reduced the hospital's income at a time when major rebuilding and repair was desperately needed.

In 1702 the main gate was rebuilt in a characteristic Queen Anne design by Edward Strong, nephew of Wren's master mason. Although it was reconstructed in 1834, and extra rooms added, it still looks authentic enough with giant Ionic pilasters and a central niche containing a Henry VIII statue.

In 1730 James Gibbs, who had recently completed St. Martin-in-the-Fields and the Cambridge Senate House, was appointed to remodel the hospital. Money was raised by public subscription and endowment – anyone who gave five guineas a year was entitled to attend the board of governors for that year, while large donations guaranteed life membership. Many people were attracted by this aura of respectability, and as his contribution Gibbs gave his architectural services for nothing.

Gibbs's design consisted of a large courtyard surrounded by four big detached blocks, with an arch through one side. The style is solid and stately with Palladian details, similar to Gibbs's Fellows Building at King's College, Cambridge. Bath stone was used, one of the earliest examples in London. Although the south-east side was demolished and rebuilt in 1935 as the George V building, the other three survive. Large plane trees have grown up in the courtyard, and a fountain plays in the middle. On warm days the mobile patients can sit out and enjoy the sun and catch sight of a little of the outside world. Only the cars spoil a peaceful scene.

In the north-west administrative block is the Great Hall, a sumptuous room with a high elaborate plaster ceiling by Jean-Baptiste St. Michele, fine stained glass and a generous acoustic. The names and donations of subscribers are recorded on the wooden panelling. The wide staircase up to the Hall is flanked by two huge murals by William Hogarth, *The Pool of Bethesda* and *The Good Samaritan*. As a governor of the hospital he painted them as a gift in 1735–6. Although somewhat inspired by Raphael, they contain all the trademarks of Hogarth's genius.

In 1789 the church of St. Bartholomew-the-Less was rebuilt by George Dance. Of the fifteenth-century building in which Inigo Jones had been baptized, only the tower and vestry were kept. Dance's design, which was incorporated in Philip Hardwick's restoration in 1834, is an unusual octagonal shape, but it is a small and friendly building, meticulously decorated and cleaned. The walls are dotted with memorials to great doctors, although one plaque is to Lady Anne Bodley, whose husband founded Oxford's famous library.

Gibbs's work was completed in 1759 and increased the number of hospital beds to 504. The number of admissions grew rapidly, to 3000 in 1760 with 300 out-patients each week. St. Bartholomew's was now as up-to-date as any hospital in the world, but conditions were still primitive by modern standards. One in thirteen of all patients admitted in 1775 died in hospital; smallpox and typhoid were incurable and

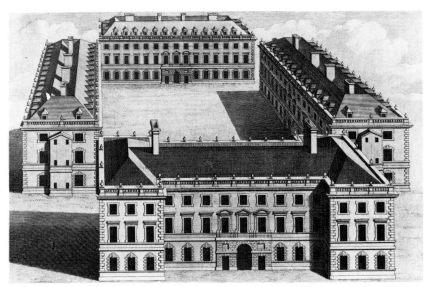

major killers until Edward Jenner's breakthrough in vaccination in 1796. Hygiene was neglected and misunderstood – windows were kept closed and the wooden beds were lice-infested; vermin catchers fought a losing battle. It is amazing that anyone was ever cured at all, until one remembers that living conditions in the home, particularly in the rookeries, were far worse.

Control over patients was lax and nurses, who were an uncouth rabble, did little more than try to keep order in the wards and dish up food. Patients who were "found strolling about the streets, or frequenting publick houses or brandy shops" lost a day's food, or if caught drinking in hospital were discharged whether they were better or not! Many returned promptly to Gin Lane. It is arguable that more valuable work was done by the General Dispensary in Aldersgate, which provided medicines and advice to out-patients.

Standards of surgery improved slowly; Bart's started teaching courses in anatomy in 1738 and a new lecture theatre was built by Dance in 1791. Until the introduction of anaesthetics in the nineteenth century and antiseptic surgery by Joseph Lister in the 1860s, operations remained a crude and chancy business. Up to 1800, surgeons were organised as a livery company, and for a long time were linked with the barbers. Surgeons had to learn their skills by dissecting criminals' bodies at Hicks Hall, for example, or by relying on the notorious practice of body-snatching. The Fortune of War tavern which stood opposite the hospital on the corner of Giltspur Street and Cock Lane, until demolished in 1910, was a favourite haunt of the resurrectionists. The exhumed bodies were laid out by the landlord on benches in an upstairs room, each labelled with the snatcher's name, waiting for the surgeons at Bart's to rush across and

James Gibbs's design for re-building the hospital, 1730. Three sides of the court survive. **Museum of London**

A pleasant refuge in the middle of so many buildings. **Theo Bergström**

103

appraise them.

Knowledge and techniques improved immensely in the nineteenth century, with great advances in surgery, gynaecology, etc., but not so great that people relished the prospect of admission to hospital. In 1805, Moorfields Eye Hospital was founded in Charterhouse Square (it later moved to a larger site in City Road). The Royal College of Surgeons began to tighten its requirements for membership in the 1830s, and actually introduced examinations. Doctors continued to be able to enjoy extensive spare time activities, however. Robert Bridges, a house surgeon from 1870 to 1882, was Poet Laureate; W. G. Grace was able to find time to earn immortality on the cricket field, while still practising a respectable medical career at the hospital. More recently, Richard Gordon, who trained at Bart's, has been very successful with his *Doctor* books and novels on aspects of medical history. Some men, such as Sir James Paget, remained devoted to the hospital and its welfare throughout their lives, while others exported their skills. Dr. Edward Wilson trained at Bart's in the 1890s and was doctor on the ill-fated trip to the South Pole in 1912 where he heroically died together with Oates, Evans and Captain Scott.

Nursing at last became a valued profession. Traditionally, nurses were coarse drunken women with thick heads and hard hands, lacking any training or instruction. In 1877, Bart's started a training course for nurses which gradually grew from humble beginnings into a fine nursing school, which it remains today. So the battle-axe image began to fade.

The number of patients escalated; out-patients quadrupled between 1832 and 1855, and doubled again by 1900. More buildings were required and duly built; these included the Medical Library (1879), the Pathological block (1907) and the Out-patients building (1909), all facing Giltspur Street and designed by L'Anson. In 1901, the hospital was electrified throughout, which greatly facilitated sterilization and heating. Such was the demand for space and new buildings that in 1904 the St. Bartholomew's Act granted powers to demolish the church of St. Bartholomew-the-Less and amalgamate it with St. Bartholomew-the-Great. Fortunately this parliamentary authority was never implemented.

Expansion continued between the wars and again afterwards. Queen Mary's nurses' home, fronting Little Britain, was built in 1921, and the Medical College moved into the former site of Merchant Taylor's School on the north side of Charterhouse Square in the mid-1930s where a series of rather faceless functional laboratories, lecture theatres and residential blocks have been erected around the grass quadrangle. East of Little Britain there are several post-war hospital buildings, such as the Queen Elizabeth wards and Gloucester House nurses' home. None of these buildings are inspired pieces of architecture, and certainly fall short of the standards set by Gibbs,

Just inside the main gate stands the medieval tower of St. Bartholomew-the-Less, so nearly demolished in 1904. **Theo Bergström**

Dance and L'Anson.

Today Bart's is one of the main teaching and research hospitals in London. Well over 2,500 people work at the hospital, including doctors, nurses, technicians, clerical and administrative officers, as well as all the ancillary workers such as porters, cleaners and canteen staff. The most important change in the last decade has been the incorporation of Bart's into the National Health Service. Traditionally Bart's was a privately-run charitable hospital for London's poor, with its own independent financial resources and board of governors. Endowments and gifts of land and money over the centuries had ensured that Bart's was comparatively wealthy and well equipped, rather like the older Oxford and Cambridge colleges.

Bart's is now part of the City and Hackney Area Health Authority and has to share its resources of staff and money with several other hospitals in the district, such as St. Leonard's. Bart's still has some degree of independence and the trustees continue to administer the private income and interests, but often this has to go in making up reduced government grants.

Despite the national and international reputation of Bart's for its research and educational functions, and the high calibre of its specialists, it is also very much a 'people's hospital', providing everyday care for the local population. The health district has a resident population of about 212,000, but in reality the local catchment is far greater, because of the large numbers of city commuters and the service that the hospital has always given to Islington and Camden residents who live nearby, but who are technically in a different health district. The removal of the Royal Free Hospital, from Gray's Inn Road to Hampstead, has increased their reliance on St. Bartholomew's.

Bart's seems to have won the battle against the threat of decentralising its teaching capacity. The Greater London Development Plan had questioned why so many medical education institutions – Guy's, St. Thomas's, St. Mary's, Westminster, Middlesex and Bart's – should be concentrated in central London, where land is expensive and scarce. Fortunately, the plans for a relocation *en masse* have been shelved. Without doubt, the loss of the teaching faculty would have been a damaging blow to the traditions and standard of medicine at Bart's.

Far from contracting, Bart's is constantly seeking to improve and strengthen its position as a specialist and research establishment, as well as hoping to increase the total number of hospital beds from 820 to 880 by 1986. Laboratory facilities are desperately overcrowded and could occupy an extra 7,000 square feet each year if the money and space were available. New accommodation for the Medical Oncology Department has recently been built in Little Britain, and Dominion House in Bartholomew Close, owned by the hospital, may be developed before long.

Inevitably, the upkeep and renovation of the older wards in the main part of the hospital consume frighteningly large amounts of money. Many ancillary facilities are also needed, such as a new laundry (at present in Swanley, Kent), a central sterile supplies unit, and a sub-regional blood transfusion centre. These could possibly occupy some of the empty industrial or cold store buildings near the hospital on the north side of the market. More residential accommodation and parking facilities are urgently required. The hospital still houses 200 nurses in hostels in the West End, at great expense and inconvenience. In the medical college there is enormous competition for rooms in the halls of residence, hardly surprising when private flats and public transport are so dear in London. Perhaps the City Corporation and London Borough of Islington could assist more by allowing nurses and students to live in the Barbican and other council flats, even if they do not qualify under the normal allocation system. The prestige of Bart's will always attract the top doctors and surgeons; it is at the more unglamorous level – trainee nurses, registrars and domestic workers – where they may soon have a staffing problem.

Parking, too, is increasingly difficult. Many staff work unsocial hours or may have to attend clinics at several different hospitals in one day, and need a car to travel quickly. If another car park could be found, perhaps all vehicles except ambulances could be expelled from the main square inside the hospital, leaving it as a pedestrian precinct.

Clearly Bart's is a vital part of Smithfield and if other activities in the area decline, the expansion of the hospital will be very welcome, so long as new buildings are sensitively designed to blend with and enhance the historic character of the area. Bart's is a flourishing community within the whole community, and contributes immensely to the life of the area – from formal open days and fund-raising fêtes (like the revival of Bartholomew Fair), to carousing medical students celebrating or drowning their sorrows in the Bishop's Finger. Let us hope that Smithfield continues to be its home.

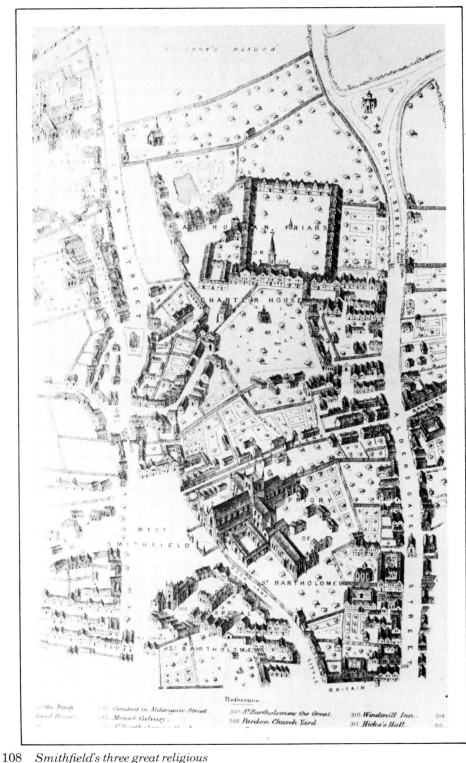

108 *Smithfield's three great religious houses in 1400; the vast church of St. Bartholomew, the cloister of The Charterhouse, and, top left, St. John's Priory.* **Finsbury Library**

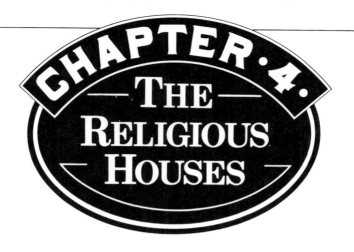

CHAPTER·4· — THE — RELIGIOUS HOUSES

In the early Middle Ages monastic institutions began to flourish in London. Their land requirements were extensive and for this reason they usually had to look outside the confines of the city wall. Three religious houses were established around Smithfield where the land was high and well drained, unlike the Fleet valley or the marshy area to the east known as Moorfields, and where there was a good supply of drinking water from springs.

THE PRIORY OF ST. BARTHOLOMEW'S

The legend of minstrel Rahere's pilgrimage to Rome, his illness, prayers and promises, his visitation by St. Bartholomew in a dream and his return to England as a chastened man, intent on founding a priory and hospital at Smithfield, lacks documentary evidence, and probably displays the fanciful embellishments of a good yarn. What is certain is that the priory and hospital were founded in 1123, the land having been given by Henry I in the previous year, and that Rahere was the first canon and prior. Indeed, far from being the king's jester and minstrel, Rahere may have in fact previously been no more than a church cleric at St. Paul's Cathedral.

Rahere was responsible for the construction of the great church and its associated monastic buildings, and although only a small amount of his prodigious feat remains, the surviving church of St. Bartholomew-the-Great is a marvellous tribute to his endeavour. Rahere died in 1143, before his project was completed, and was buried in the church; his tomb is surmounted by a sixteenth-century stone effigy. The simplicity of the Latin inscription – "Here lies Rahere, the first canon and first prior of this church" – probably saved it from the wrath of Reformation and Cromwellian iconoclasts. Sadly, Rahere's tomb was broken into in 1866 and some of his remains were stolen.

Only part of the original church survives – the chancel, crossing, transepts and lady chapel – yet these alone make up a very sizeable building. The original church was colossal, about 300 feet long with the nave extending right through to the Smithfield frontage where the great west door faced onto the open space. This massive church was then larger than Rochester, Bristol or Chester cathedrals, and the huge columns at the crossing supported a tall central tower, until it was struck by lightning in 1264. Because of settlement problems it was not rebuilt. The lower stones of the thirteenth-century west door survive in the arch of the present-day gateway which leads into the churchyard. The upper storeys of the gateway are half-timbered – heavily restored but nevertheless very picturesque. Curiously this timberwork, built in 1559, was only revealed when tiles and stucco facings were dislodged by a Zeppelin raid in 1916.

South of the nave were the cloisters, only one arm of which still survives. The remaining eight bays (once there were thirty-nine) were used as stables until the early 1900s when they were carefully restored and the original cloister doors, removed during the dissolution, were rehung in their rightful place. The centre of the old cloisters is now a small grass square used by one of the childrens' wards in the hospital.

The Augustinian priory prospered throughout the thirteenth, fourteenth and fifteenth centuries, supporting the hospital but also accumulating great wealth. The church was a place of refuge, not that this was always respected; in 1381 the injured Wat Tyler was unceremoniously dragged from the church and beheaded outside. Bartholomew Fair belonged to the Priory, and was originally held on church land although it quickly grew beyond the churchyard. The fair which was licensed for three days, August 23rd–25th, produced a lot of income for the prior, much to the chagrin of the jealous city authorities.

A large manorial estate was amassed in Islington, and gave the area its name, Canonbury. One of the last and most famous of St. Bartholomew's priors, Prior Bolton, built the tall brick tower which stands on the corner of Canonbury Place and Alwyne Villas. William Bolton, prior from 1509 to 1532, was reputedly worried by popular prognostications that a conjunction of astrological water signs would bring a cataclysmic flood in 1524. To ensure his survival, he built in true Noah-fashion a house on top of Harrow-on-the-Hill as well as the Canonbury Tower, and stocked them with enough provisions to last two months' isolation. Whatever his eccentricities, Bolton was a great builder, and made several repairs and alterations to the priory church, including the beautiful oriel window in the south ambulat-

Fred. Adcock.

ory. This also shows his rebus, which is a visual pun on his name – an arrow or 'bolt' piercing a barrel or 'tun'.

The wealth of the priory made it a prime target for dissolution, and it was duly closed down in October 1539, and all the land, buildings and possessions, including 1,300 ounces of gold plate, were confiscated. Prior Fuller, who had succeeded Bolton, meekly raised no objection, and as a reward for his complicity received a pension of

In the nineteenth century a cooper's yard occupied the cloisters. The lady chapel was leased to printers and the north transept housed a blacksmith's forge! **G.L.C.**

£200, although he only lived another nine months and so had little time to enjoy it!

The dismantling of the priory was entrusted by Henry VIII to Sir Richard Rich who decided that the nave of the church should be demolished, leaving the chancel as a parish church, to which a rector was duly appointed. The lead from the roof of the nave was melted down and sold, and six of the eleven bells taken to St. Sepulchre's. The five remaining bells, cast in about 1520, survive and are still rung for

The lovely tower and west door of St. Bartholomew-the-Great, a mellow blend of stone, flint and brick.
Theo Bergström

Sunday evensong, London's oldest peal. Rich himself took up residence in the prior's house and in 1544 became the owner. The site of the nave became the parish graveyard, which it still is today. Rich converted the lady chapel, which had been built in 1330, into a private house, and sold off some of the cloisters to Sir Walter Mildmay who built his house there. Mildmay founded Emmanuel College, Cambridge, and was Chancellor of the Exchequer to Elizabeth I by the time he died in 1589; his memorial stands in the church. In 1740

Bolton's window, with his 'bolt' and
'tun' rebus, built in 1517 by the
eccentric prior to observe mass without
having to enter the church.
Theo Bergström

Mildmay's house was converted into a tavern, known as the Flying Horse, derived from Mildmay's coat-of-arms.

In 1628, the church tower was rebuilt in red brick and stone, and surmounted with a little wooden lantern and weather vane. However, there was little other improvement and other uses began to impinge on the church. By about 1720, the lady chapel had been converted into a factory, and the third floor was occupied by a printer, where in 1725 Benjamin Franklin worked as an apprentice. By the nineteenth century the factory had expanded into part of the apse and was used for making cloth fringes. The old north transept was blocked off and leased out as a blacksmith's forge fronting Cloth Fair; the anvil's hammer could be heard loud and clear in church.

Parish life bumbled along, and in November, 1697, William Hogarth was baptised in the church, using the fifteenth-century font, which today is one of only two pre-reformation fonts left in London. Whereas most London churches had benefited from complete rebuilding or substantial repair in the eighteenth century, following the Fire of London, St. Bartholomew's was untouched by the Wrens, Gibbses, Archers and Hawksmoors of the time. Gradually its condition deteriorated, and had it not been for tremendous restoration works at the end of the nineteenth century, the dilapidated church might have been lost.

Virtually the whole church was overhauled and about £40,000 was spent over twenty-five years, master-minded by the architect Sir Aston Webb and supported by the rector Borradaile Savory. In 1890–1 the south transept, which had lost its roof, was restored, and in 1893 a new west porch, north transept and north porch facing were added, all by Aston Webb. In 1897 the lady chapel was re-acquired and restored while the outside walls were patched up, mainly with flint. Inside, a new organ case, choir and lady chapel screens were installed. In 1895 access to the crypt underneath the lady chapel was gained by opening up the old bone chute which the monks had once used to bury their dead. The crypt is very damp and only usable in dry weather.

Purists may not particularly care for these extensive nineteenth-century renovations, but on the whole the blend of old and modern is extremely successful, and has retained and enhanced the calm dignity of the original Norman church. St. Bartholomew-the-Great is London's oldest parish church; only the chapel of St. John in the Tower of London has older ecclesiastical fabric.

St. Bartholomew's today is an extraordinary amalgam of styles and periods. The square brick tower and the flint and freestone walls give the outside of the church an almost East Anglian appearance, while the interior is surely one of the most majestic of any building in London. The dark stone, the magnificent Norman pillars and round arches of the chancel, apse and triforium, are worthy of the noblest monastic architecture of the age. Here is an austere beauty and tranquillity which is unique in London.

The church is a honeycomb of unexpected nooks and crannies and a jumble of curiosities. Some of the monuments and memorials are quite amusing. One to Margaret and John Whiting, who died in 1681, reads:

"Shee first deceased, Hee for a little Tryd
To live without her, likd it not and dyd."

Another to Edward Cooke (died 1652) is carved on a stone which was once said to shed tears. No drops have been seen since a radiator was installed immediately below it. The only memorial to Aston Webb, who did so much to restore the church to its present condition, is in the old gateway fronting onto Smithfield which was renovated in 1932, but the church itself is a fitting monument to his work.

Compared to many other London churches, St. Bartholomew's is amazingly little known and only attracts the adventurous or well-informed sightseer — which maybe is a blessing. In the last few years the church has been used increasingly for concerts, and it now holds its own festival. With reasonable acoustics, a good seating capacity, as well as the architectural surroundings, this festival has been a great success.

The churchyard, now disused but dotted with eighteenth and nineteenth century gravestones, is a pleasant quiet space; perhaps the area south of the lady chapel facing Bartholomew Close could also be made into a small sunken garden and so perfect the setting for Rahere's great church.

ST. JOHN'S PRIORY

North of the meat market, a short distance up St. John's Lane is St. John's Gateway which, together with the crypt and chancel of the church on the other side of the square, is the only surviving fabric of the old priory of St. John. This priory, founded shortly after the priory of St. Bartholomew's, was not a purely monastic institution. It was built to provide a home and recruitment centre for the Knights of the Hospital of St. John of Jerusalem, who had established themselves as a religious military order during the crusades in the Holy Land at the end of the eleventh century. By 1140 the order had taken roots in England, and owned among others the village of Shingay in Cambridgeshire.

In 1144 a rich Anglo-Norman land owner, Jordan de Briset, gave fifteen acres of land at Clerkenwell to the Church to be divided between the Knights Hospitallers and a new nunnery called St. Mary's. After some bickering over acreages, Jordan de Briset mediated by allocating ten acres to St. Mary's and five to St. John's.

The first Prior, Walter, began building in 1148 – a large rectangular courtyard roughly on the lines of present-day St. John's Square, with a southern gateway, a church and domestic buildings. Apart from the Gate and church it has been difficult to locate any archaeological remains of the other monastic buildings, although a few fragments of walling have been found during excavation works in St. John's Square.

The church was modelled on the Church of the Holy Sepulchre in Jerusalem, with its distinctive round nave. The original outline is marked by cobblestones set in the paving and tarmac in St. John's Square. A few churches belonging to the Order were built in this fashion, and the Knights Templar, who had settled beside the River Thames in 1161, also imitated the Holy Sepulchre Church. These two organisations were responsible for most of the circular churches in England. Only a few survive and even then they are often spurious rebuilds, like the Round Church in Cambridge.

Prior Walter's church was consecrated in 1185 by the Patriarch of Jerusalem, Heraclius, who was visiting England to raise support for the wars against the Turks. He even tried to persuade Henry II to lead a crusade, and the priory was the setting for their famous confrontation. Henry was advised by his barons to stay at home, and the incensed Heraclius daringly rebuked the king:

"We come to seek a king, not money, for every corner of the world sends us money but not one a prince. Here is my head; treat me if you like as you did my brother (i.e. Thomas à Becket); it matters little to me whether I die by your orders or in Syria by the hands of the infidels, for you are worse than a Saracen!"

Surprisingly, Henry kept his cool and Heraclius kept his head.

As the headquarters of the Order, St. John's Priory was a very important national institution and at times was very wealthy. In 1312, the Knights Templar were disbanded, having been accused of heresy and witchcraft; all their property, including that on the north bank of the river, was handed to the Order of St. John, who leased it to a group of lawyers. The lawyers have stayed there ever since. Part of the estate was a large plantation a few miles away in Middlesex in open country, which we know today as St. John's Wood, and they also owned the manors at Highbury and Chingford, Purfleet, Witham and Temple Rhodon in Essex.

St. John's Priory was noted for its hospitality to travellers, from kings and noblemen to destitute wayfarers. Dick Whittington, arriving in London in 1368 to seek his fortune but without a penny to his name, was taken in at the priory and was allowed to stay there for a while in return for his labour.

The dress of the prior and knights, a black habit with a white cross, became the renowned symbol of the defence of Christianity against

the pagans. However, the wealth and power of the priory attracted the full fury of Wat Tyler's mob in the 1381 uprising. After the destruction of the Temple and the Savoy, St. John's was looted and burnt and the wealthy prior Sir Robert Hales, known as Hobbe the Robber, was chased to the Tower where he was dragged out and beheaded on Tower Hill. Hales was Chancellor of the Realm and responsible for gathering the tax which sparked off the rebellion. Another of the rebel leaders, Jack Straw, ransacked the Highbury Manor.

Prior Hales' successor, John Redington, began rebuilding and by 1399 the priory was sufficiently restored to accommodate Henry IV for two weeks before his coronation in London. In 1485 Richard III chose the priory as a suitable venue to summon all the great English barons and London dignitaries in order to announce his matrimonial plans.

The church was reconstructed in perpendicular style with a rectangular nave, ninety feet long with a bell tower in the north-west corner. The old Norman crypt was kept, however, having been un-affected by the plundering rebels. Restoration continued under Thomas Docwra, who was prior from 1501 to 1527. In addition to inserting the windows that survive in the church walls, he built the great gateway in 1504 which still straddles St. John's Lane. The grey ragstone and red brickwork have been heavily restored, but it remains one of London's finest ancient monuments; the astuteness and ability of Docwra is commemorated by a plaque on the underside of the archway.

The original crypt of St. John's survives from 1148, and except for the chapel in the Tower of London, is the oldest church in London.
Theo Bergström

118 *Docwra's famous Gate, recently cleaned; an
impressive sight, despite the cars and buildings.
Vehicles have now been banished from under the
Gate, and the old granite setts exposed.*
Theo Bergström

When Henry VIII embarked on a programme to suppress and dissolve monasteries from 1535 onwards, the priory's future was placed in serious jeopardy. By 1538 even the biggest monasteries were under fire and in the autumn of 1539, the last and greatest of all, Glastonbury, surrendered. The Knights of St. John were of superior ilk compared to 'run of the mill' monks and nuns, but were nevertheless loyal servants of the Pope. Their position grew increasingly embarrassing and then intolerable to Henry, who was self-anointed supreme head of the Church of England. In 1540 the inevitable happened – the Order was dissolved, its estates confiscated and transferred to the Crown, and the uniform of white cross on black background banned.

The wealth of the priory surpassed any other religious house in London. The Temple was leased off to the lawyers in perpetuity, St. John's Wood became a royal hunting park, and the priory buildings were soon occupied by other uses. The shock dissolution is said to have broken the heart of Prior William Weston, who had succeeded Docwra, and he died in May 1540, on the very day that the king's command took effect. His effigy, a gruesomely emaciated skeleton, lies on his tomb in the church crypt. A few troublesome members of the Order were martyred and the remaining knights, who refused to recognise the king, fled to Malta where the Order had been settled for ten years. Malta remained the headquarters of the Knights of St. John until conquered by Napoleon in 1798. After Henry's death, serious efforts were made to re-establish the English Order at St. John's Priory under Edward VI and Queen Mary, but neither reign lasted long enough, and in 1559 Elizabeth I finally quashed the move.

During the 1540s the church and outbuildings were used for storing Henry's hunting equipment and tents but in 1550 the Duke of Somerset, Protector to the young Edward VI, blew up the church with gunpowder and took the stone to build his palace in the Strand, Somerset House, though he was beheaded before it was completed. Stow records the event with some nostalgia, mourning the loss of the great belfry tower – "a most curious piece of workmanship, graven, gilt and enamelled, to the great beautifying of the city, and passing all other that I have seen".

The more settled Elizabethan era saw the Gateway converted into the offices and home of the Master of Revels, Edmund Tilney, who was responsible for licensing all plays for public performance, rather like the public censor today. William Shakespeare would almost certainly have visited St. John's Gate many times on business, armed with his latest play ready for production at the Globe Theatre. The staircase in the east wing of the gate was widened and replaced in a fine Jacobean style. Most of the rest of the priory was given to the Earls of Aylesbury who built their country house there. The remnants of the church were used as the family chapel, with a library extended on the north side, while the old crypt proved an ideal wine cellar. West of the gateway Sir Maurice Berkeley, standard bearer to four monarchs from 1530 to 1570, built a fine brick mansion for his London home.

In the seventeenth century the Aylesburys sold up and the buildings fell into disuse and disrepair. Following the Fire of London Smithfield and Clerkenwell absorbed a huge influx of population, and many workshops and small industries sprang up around the square. The Gate became one of London's fashionable coffee houses, which from the Restoration of Charles II were very popular centres for London social life. Although tobacco and spirits were sold, coffee houses afforded some respite from the heavy alcoholism of the time. Every respectable Londoner had his favourite place, where business and social meetings could be arranged side by side and where news-sheets and magazines could be bought. In the early 1700s William Hogarth's father was proprietor at the St. John's Gate, and was "always ready to entertain gentlemen in the Latin tongue".

Other buildings around St. John's Square were pulled down to make way for fine Georgian houses by Simon Michell, who also developed Britton Street. St. John's Square became a smart address and residents included the eminent and candid Bishop Burnet. In 1721 the ruins of the church, part of which had been used as a presbyterian chapel, were bought by the church commissioners and restored with money given by Simon Michell. With a new west front and elegant wooden galleries and pews, St. John's church became a second parish church for Clerkenwell to relieve the overcrowded St. James's church in 1723.

St. John's remained a parish church until 1929 when population decline made two churches unnecessary. Until the late nineteenth century the crypt was used for parish burials, simply because there was no graveyard and no alternative. In 1894, it was decided that the crypt should be cleaned out and the bones removed to a new cemetery which had been bought at Woking. The cost of moving the 300 lead coffins and scraping out the decomposing human mould, which lay three feet deep, was £750. This created a tremendous hullabaloo when it was charged on the rates. The furious ratepayers took the church commissioners and local council to court, but despite vehement protests, they lost. No doubt they carried their grudge to the next election.

Meanwhile, the gate in 1731 had become the home of Edward Cave, where for the next fifty years the *Gentleman's Magazine* was edited, printed and published. Edward Cave, born in Rugby in 1691, was a large phlegmatic man, an abstemious vegetarian and teetotaller, whose only exercise was an occasional game of shuttlecock in a room over the gate. *The Gentleman's Magazine or Monthly Intelligencer* was Cave's brainchild, and the front cover retained a picture of the St.

John's Gate from the first edition in January, 1731, right through to the 1890s, even though the centre of operations had by then long since moved elsewhere.

The magazine's most celebrated contributor was Dr. Samuel Johnson. The magazine had attracted the notice and esteem of Johnson before he came to London as a literary adventurer. In 1736 Johnson actually used the paper to advertise his school:

> "At EDIAL, near Lichfield, in Staffordshire, young gentlemen are boarded and taught the Latin and Greek languages by SAMUEL JOHNSON."

When he arrived in London in 1737, Johnson promptly applied to Cave for work, submitting a flattering Latin verse, "in so happy a style of compliment that Cave must have been both destitute of taste and sensibility had he not felt himself highly gratified." Johnson was enlisted as a regular coadjutor. Boswell also records that Johnson when he first saw St. John's Gate "beheld it with reverence", but maybe not because of its architecture; "I suppose that every young author has had the same kind of feeling for the magazine or periodical which has first entertained him."

Writing under the pseudonym of "The Senate of Lilliput", Johnson's reports of parliamentary debates were pioneering journalism. At that time, Parliament liked to keep the press and public in the dark as much as possible, and Johnson's reports were a mixture of imaginative fabrication and a thinly disguised political commentary, using anagrams for the names of well-known statesmen in order to evade breach of privilege. Johnson scraped a meagre living; Cave

Removing the bones from the crypt in 1894. Before then the lack of a graveyard left no alternative to the crypt for burials. **Finsbury Library**

The Gentleman's Magazine:

St John's Gate.

Lond.Gazette
Londo. Jour.
Fog's Journ.
Applebee's ::
Read's ::::
Craftsman ::
O. Spectator
Grubstreet J.
Wkly Register
Free-Briton.
Imp. Doctor
Daily Courant
Daily Post.:
Dai. Journal
Dai.Post-boy
D. Advertiser
Evening Post
St James's Ev.
Whitehall Ev.
Lodon Eveng
Flying-Post

York Journals
Dublin ditto
Edinburgh 2
Norwich two
Exeter two:
Worcester 2.:
Northampto
Gloucester ::
Stamford ::
Nottingham
Bristol News
Bury Journ.
Ipswich do.
Chester ditto
Leeds Merc.
Newcastle C.
Derby Journ.
Reading ditto
Canterbury
Boston : : : b
Jamaica, &c.

Or, Monthly Intelligencer.

NUMBER I. for JANUARY, 1731.

CONTAINING,

/more in Quantity, and greater Variety, than any Book of the Kind and Price/

I. A View of the Weekly *Essays* and *Controversies*, viz. Of Q. *Elizabeth* ; Ministers ; Treaties ; Liberty of the Press ; Riot Act ; Armies ; Traytors ; Patriots ; Reason ; Criticism ; Versifying ; Ridicule ; Humours ; Love ; Prostitutes ; Music ; Pawn-brokers ; Surgery ; Law.

II. POETRY, *viz.* The Ode for the New Year, by *Colly Cibber*, Esq; Remarks upon it ; Imitations of it, by way of *Burlesque* ; Verses on the same Subject ; ingenious Epitaphs and Epigrams.

III. *Domestick* Occurrences, *viz.* Births,

Births, Deaths, Marriages, Preferments, Casualties, Burials and Christenings in *London*.

IV. Melancholy Effects of Credulity in *Witchcraft*.

V. Prices of Goods and Stocks, and a List of Bankrupts.

VI. A correct List of the Sheriffs for the current Year.

VII. Remarkable *Advertisements*.

VIII. *Foreign* Affairs, with an Introduction to this Year's History.

IX. Books and Pamphlets publish'd.

X. Observations on *Gardening*, and a List of Fairs for the Season.

With a *Table* of Contents.

By *SYLVANUS URBAN*, Gent.

The FOURTH EDITION.

LONDON, Printed and Sold at *St John's Gate*; by F. *Jefferies* in *Ludgate-street*; and most Booksellers in Town and Country. 1732. (Price 6 d.)

Note, *A few are printed on fine* Royal Paper, *large Margin, for the Curious*.

The front page of the first edition. This format lasted for 160 years.
Finsbury Library

insisted that he eat behind a screen to hide his shabby clothes from well-to-do visitors at the Gate. Despite this meanness, Cave and Johnson were close friends and when Cave died in 1754, he was "pressing gently into Johnson's hand" (Boswell). However, by 1745, Johnson was branching out and soon no longer needed to do hack work for the magazine. He started his great dictionary in 1747 and took up more salubrious residence in Gough Square on the other side of the Fleet River.

During Johnson's time at the Gate, Oliver Goldsmith was a frequent visitor, being a mutual friend of his and Cave's, and living nearby opposite the Old Bailey. Another auspicious visitor was the young David Garrick who had accompanied Johnson to London, and who, apart from his brother George, had been Johnson's only pupil at Lichfield (hence the advertisement)! At the Gate Garrick, the budding actor, was tried out, playing a comic part from Fielding's *Mock Doctor*, with some of Cave's printers filling in the other parts. In 1741, Garrick made his public debut in *Richard III* and was an instant success. For the next thirty-five years he dominated the London stage with his new style of naturalistic acting, particularly in Shakespearian roles. He became actor-manager of the Drury Lane Theatre in 1747, where he followed a triumphant career.

When the *Gentleman's Magazine* moved to new premises the Gate became a public house, the Old Jerusalem Tavern, but it was badly neglected, so much so that by 1845 it was derelict and in danger of collapsing. The tavern moved into next door premises, where it remained until it closed in 1914. (There is now a modern pub in St. John Street with the same name.) Money was raised by public subscription to save the Gate and restoration was carried out by

In 1828 the Gate was occupied by the Old Jerusalem Tavern, and in poor condition. The brick kiln next door disappeared in the following year.
Finsbury Library

William Pettit Griffith, a local architect, and the Gate put up for sale.

In 1831 the Order of St. John, was reconstituted in England within the framework of the Church of England, strict humanitarian objectives replacing the original Catholic fervour. In 1869, the Order was represented at the International Conference of the Red Cross. By 1880 the Order had established an ambulance service, and so began the St. John Ambulance Brigade, for which the Order is best known today to the general public.

In 1874 the Gate was bought for the Order, and so by an extraordinary chain of events an Order of St. John returned to the original home of the Hospitallers of St. John of 730 years before. By 1888 the Order had gained such respect that Queen Victoria granted a Royal Charter, and the Order has enjoyed the most cordial ecumenical relations with the Sovereign ever since.

The gateway was further restored and in 1903 the buildings were extended by John Oldrid Scott, second son of the famous Sir George Gilbert Scott. The new chapter house on the south-east side of the Gate was designed in a traditional gothic style, faced in ragstone to match the Gate, and with dark sombre wood panelling and roof timbers inside. Scott also restored the council chamber directly above the archway, and inserted the beautiful Whitefriars stained glass in the main windows over the Gate. A sixteenth-century fireplace was rescued from an old house in St. John's Lane which was being demolished and fitted into the east tower chancery.

Today the Gate and chapter house hold many of the most treasured possessions of the Order of St. John. These include a fine collection of eighteenth-century Maltese silver cups, plates and boxes (mostly obtained when the English recaptured Malta in 1840), a lovely French silver cross from 1527, still used in processions, numerous medals and crusader coins struck by various Grand Masters of the Order in Jerusalem, Rhodes and Malta, usually featuring the head of John the Baptist, and some ornate seventeenth- and eighteenth-century French and Spanish furniture. The library in the west tower contains ancient statutes of the Order including many editions of Bosio's history, but the prize is the Rhodes Missal, written and illuminated by the Prior of Provence as a gift to the Grand Master in Rhodes in 1502. On this manuscript, exquisitely adorned in rich colours with birds, butterflies, fruit and flowers, the Knights swore their allegiance. Rows of portraits of former grand masters of the Order line the walls of the chapter house and east tower staircase. With a fine collection of armour, model ships, stonework from the old priory, photographs and historic Brigade equipment, a fascinating museum has at last been opened on the ground floor of the chapter house. The gateway itself is of course well worth a visit; perhaps the finest feature is the rare wooden spiral staircase in the four-storey west tower, unaltered since 1504, maybe because it has always been

*The chapter house, setting for the
pageants and ceremonies of today's
Order.*   **Theo Bergström**

126 *Banners from great military victories;*
shields of previous Grand Masters.
Theo Bergström

the 'back stairs'.

In 1929, the parish church of St. John's became surplus to requirements and was bought in 1931 by the Order. The nave was blitzed in 1941 and rebuilt in the 1950s by Lord Mottistone in a very plain manner – a whitewashed rectangular hall with a simple flat roof and unassuming brick facade onto St. John's Square. Behind the altar are two panels of the triptych given to the priory church in 1480 by Prior John Weston. Although the centre portion has never been found, the side panels were miraculously preserved after 1540 in Milton Abbey, Dorset, and retrieved by the Order in 1932.

The twelfth-century rib-vaulted crypt has survived everything, and is a cool quiet sanctuary from the noise of Clerkenwell Road. It contains a fine alabaster effigy, elaborately dressed in armour, of a Spaniard, Don Juan Ruiz de Vergara, who died in 1567. Interestingly, only fifty years ago the crypt was thought to be eleventh century, for when it was built in about 1150 a very conservative Norman style was used. The old cannon which once stood in the cloister garden beside the church has been moved into the museum. Given by Henry VIII in 1522 to assist the recovery of Rhodes, the gun lay in Famagusta harbour from 1570 to 1907 when it was fished out by a sponge diver.

Pro fide, pro utilitate hominium is the Order's motto, and is fulfilled in the two charitable foundations run by the Order today. The St. John Ambulance Brigade and Association spreads the knowledge and practice of first-aid and provides voluntary services in the field; over one-quarter of a million men and women at home and overseas are members. The St. John Ophthalmic Hospital in Jerusalem, founded in 1882 and rebuilt in 1960, provides free medical treatment serving the whole Middle East. The Order depends entirely on subscriptions and legacies and dispenses about £1 million each year.

In 1962, a new building was erected on the west side of the Gate to house the Stores Department which supplies stretchers, bandages, handbooks etc. The design of Priory House, four storeys high, level with the Gate and with unsympathetic features, was approved by the

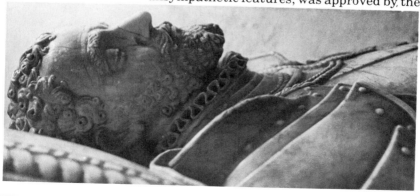

Don Juan Ruiz de Vergora, at rest in the crypt, far from his native Spain.
Theo Bergström

127

Royal Fine Arts Commission. The setting of the Gate has certainly suffered because of Priory House and other redevelopment in the square. Perhaps it was not too bad for 1962 when English architecture was at a particularly low ebb; one would like to think that the 1970s might have produced something better.

As the Headquarters of the Order, the Gate has many distinguished visitors especially for ceremonial investitures – the Duke of Gloucester is the present Grand Prior. In 1968 the Queen became the first reigning monarch to visit the Gate since Henry VIII in 1528. The gateway was immaculately cleaned in 1977 (at a cost of £30,000) and must now look as it did before nineteenth- and twentieth-century grime blackened it. There seems no reason why the Order should not continue to prosper here for another 800 years.

THE CHARTERHOUSE

Northeast of the meat market, bounded by St. John Street, Clerkenwell Road, Goswell Road and Charterhouse Square, is a large secluded area which contains the remains of The Charterhouse. Here lies one of the most remarkable collections of historic buildings in London.

The priories of Bartholomew's and St. John's had been established two hundred years before the founding of The Charterhouse. Indeed all the land on which The Charterhouse was built had originally been owned by the priory and hospital of Bartholomew's, and was known as 'Spittle Croft'. A small part of the area was called 'No Man's Land', and had been used as a 'pardon churchyard', where thieves and desperadoes were buried – a sort of medieval Golgotha. The criminals' bodies were carried here in a simple cart, covered by a rough black sack. A bell attached to the cart rang to broadcast its approach.

In 1348 the Black Death reached London, having spread from Europe into Southern England, and in 1349, when the death toll was at its peak, thirteen acres of the Spittle Croft were bought by Sir Walter de Manny as a burial ground for the thousands of corpses which the city graveyards could no longer cope with. Probably about 30,000 people were buried in this plague pit although Stow suggests it was 50,000. The main grave in Charterhouse Square has never been built on; the roots of the giant plane trees* in the square clearly enjoy the nourishment! Next to the cemetery de Manny built a small memorial chapel for the Black Death victims and this was to become the nucleus of the monastery that he had vowed to found on the site. He achieved his ambition in 1371, just before his death, when he bought the remaining land from the hospital and provided the construction funds for a Carthusian monastery. This became known as

* A few succumbed to the mighty storm in October 1987.

The Charterhouse – a corruption of Chartreuse in France, site of the original Carthusian monastery.

Sir Walter de Manny was French-born but became a naturalised Englishman and served as a loyal and gallant soldier under Edward III, was knighted in 1331 and elevated to a baron in 1345. He was a giant of a man, with flowing red hair, and a close friend of the Black Prince; together they were renowned for their courage and chivalry in battle, particularly after their heroic exploits at Crecy where they fought against incredible odds. When Sir Walter died in January, 1372, his funeral was attended by John of Gaunt and the Black Prince.

De Manny's idea for a Carthusian monastery had been suggested by the Bishop of London, and in 1371 work started with Henry Yevele as builder. The layout followed the pattern of all Carthusian monasteries, as can be seen in the ruins of Mount Grace Priory, Yorkshire, and in the modern St. Hugh's Charterhouse at Partridge Green, Cowfold, Sussex. Our knowledge of the layout comes from the Watercourse parchment, a fifteenth-century map showing the monastery and the system of pipes bringing water down the 'white conduit' from Barnsbury hill. This piped water supply was laid in 1431 (a royal licence was needed to carry water across other people's land) and followed a similar project done by St. John's Priory.

The layout of the monastery differs from all other monastic orders owing to the Carthusians' strict ascetic discipline. The Great Cloister was the entire basis. This was a large square garden and orchard surrounded by a closed passage off which were twenty-four cells where the monks lived in virtual solitary confinement. Outside the cloister was the chapel, the laymen's quarters, and beyond – the wicked wide world. The rules of silence and seclusion to which the prior and monks subjected themselves were extremely exacting. Even their dress, an itchy hair shirt and heavy rough white habit and cowl, must have been a torment. Food was handed to them through a small opening in the cell wall by the lay brothers and conversation was forbidden. Their only communication was at mass, matins and evensong. What is more the evening service had to be sung slowly, to test the patience and strength of their souls to the limits; at Charterhouse in the fifteenth and sixteenth centuries the chanting was *molto adagio*, and would drone on long into the night. Klemperer would have been proud of them! Chaucer's monk from *The Canterbury Tales*, who sneered at study and devotion, wore a fur-lined habit and ate like a glutton, was clearly not a Carthusian. It seems unlikely that the Charterhouse monks ever indulged in making chartreuse for which the French order was famous. Their misery must have been complete.

Sir Thomas More, 'man for all seasons', having been educated at Oxford and Lincoln's Inn in classics and law, spent four years at The

The outer gate of The Charterhouse.

Looking back into Charterhouse Square.

The old water conduit house.

Around the next corner.

130

The bricked-up food hatch for beggars and lepers.

Washhouse Court, the laybrothers' quarters.

Archway to Master's Court.

Master's Court. Flint lines indicate monastic foundations.

Theo Bergström

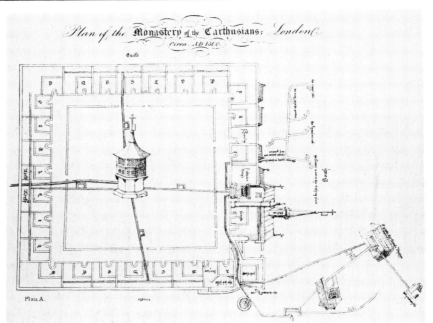

Charterhouse in frugal solitude, but he never took the vows, and returned to the dangerous political world where he became Lord Chancellor in 1529. His religious disagreement with Henry VIII sentenced him to death in 1535, but ironically he would probably have died even more horrifically had he taken vows and stayed at The Charterhouse. In 1535, Prior John Houghton and three of his monks refused to accept the king as head of the church, and were executed in the most barbaric way – dragged on hurdles to Tyburn scaffold, half-hanged and while still conscious, disembowelled, and their limbs amputated. One of Houghton's gruesome blood-spattered arms was pinned as a hideous trophy on the outer gate of The Charterhouse, to teach the man in the street a lesson and not to doubt the king. However, Prior Houghton's steadfast opposition and courage shook even the king, who had been used to cringing obedience and co-operation from most priors and abbots. Houghton and his three fellow monks were among the Forty English Martyrs canonized by the Pope in 1970.

Henry VIII, having massacred the inmates, dissolved The Charterhouse, stripped it of timber, glass and fruit trees for his Chelsea garden, and embezzled their money and land, which had included the Manor of the Blemund family, now known as Bloomsbury. After lying idle for eight years the monastic buildings were granted as a reward to Sir Edward North who had helped Henry collect the revenues from dissolved monasteries. He proceeded to demolish, rebuild and convert the premises into a comfortable country mansion.

The Watercourse parchment. Each monk had his own cell and garden. Note the water conduit house and the outer gate. **Finsbury Library**

Not much of the original monastery was kept. The chapel was largely destroyed and North used the stones to build his dining hall. The lay brothers' Washhouse Court was not demolished, however, but was adapted as servants' quarters. Tudor windows were inserted and fine brick chimneys added, but otherwise the building was unaltered. The original stone flags survive and in the outside wall is the outline of a hatch used for dispensing bread to the poor. A pile of oyster shells was discovered here – they used to be harvested from the Thames and were paupers' food in medieval times.

The outer gateway also survives, although it was extended and included as part of the gatehouse lodge in 1715. The original fourteenth-century arch remains in very good condition having been preserved under stucco until recently. The lower part of the southern

*The west side of the great cloister, with
exquisite Tudor brick vaulting.*
Theo Bergström

133

boundary wall is also monastic with its distinctive square-patterned flintwork. North demolished most of the great cloister except for the west side which he kept as a covered walkway to his tennis court and bowling green. The ceiling was subsequently rebuilt in the best Tudor style to provide an elevated roof walk on which Elizabeth I strolled during her five day stay in 1558, just before her coronation. In the eighteenth century Gainsborough painted from this vantage point. Post-war renovation uncovered one of the old entrances to a monk's cell, marked 'Cell B', in the cloister wall together with the tiny food hatch used by the lay brother which served as the monk's only link with the outside world. Also preserved was the three-storey stone tower which had been the vestibule to the chapter house with the treasure house on the first floor.

Lord North's mansion was centred round a new courtyard, Master's Court, built in ragstone rubble with ashlar dressings and fine square-headed Tudor windows. In the north range is the Great Hall; much of the original wood carving, including the noble hammer-beam roof, miraculously escaped the incendiary bombs of the war with only minor singeing. The fourteenth-century ceiling beams in the monks' old refectory were incorporated in North's kitchen. A new chapel was built using the site and materials of the former chapter house. The walls were covered in panelling and a new roof and pillars were erected.

In 1565 Lord North died and his son sold The Charterhouse to the Duke of Norfolk, and for the next forty-six years it was known as Howard House. Thomas Howard, fourth Duke, made several altera-tions, including the addition of the Elizabethan Great Chamber, or Tapestry Room, above the old refectory. The Howards' heraldry was

'Cell B'. Each monk was locked in his cell and food and water was passed through the hatch by the lay-brothers. No words were spoken.
Theo Bergström

*The Great Hall with its hammer-beam
roof and minstrels gallery.*
Theo Bergström

136   *Top left; Thomas Howard, Fourth
Duke of Norfolk, conspirator with
Ridolfi against the Queen.*

*Top right; son of the Fourth Duke,
Lord Thomas Howard, lived at*

Charterhouse 1606-1611.
Finsbury Library

*Thomas Sutton, founder of
Charterhouse School and Sutton's
Hospital.* **Finsbury Library**

embossed on the ornate ceiling. Elizabeth I was a guest at Howard House but before long Norfolk fell from grace and in 1570 he was imprisoned in the Tower for his pains, but soon released. However, the next year Ridolfi, agent of Philip of Spain, came to Howard House and he and Norfolk hatched up the Ridolfi Plot to put Mary Queen of Scots on the throne, with Norfolk as Protector. The conspiracy was exposed and Norfolk arrested, reputedly on the stairs beside the Great Hall; he was executed in 1572. Norfolk's son, the Earl of Arundel, kept Howard House but rented it to the Portuguese ambassador. In 1601 another of Norfolk's sons, Lord Thomas Howard, took up residence and in 1603 the old Queen was once again a visitor. Two months later, in May, James VI of Scotland stayed at Howard House on his way to Westminster, and was proclaimed King James I of England in the Great Chamber where he knighted his first hundred knights.

Thomas Howard lost interest in the house and in 1611 sold it to Thomas Sutton for £13,000. Sutton, born in 1532, was the richest commoner in the kingdom, having made a huge fortune as a pioneer investor in mining and shipping coal. It was rumoured that he even tried to bribe the Duke of York to give him a title. When he died in 1611, he left an endowment of £200,000 (an enormous sum in those days) to set up a charitable school for twenty-five free boy scholars and a hospice or home for eighty genteel military pensioners. So started Charterhouse School, to become one of the most famous English public schools, while the Sutton's Hospital in Charterhouse is still run on the same basis, 369 years later.

Howard House was adapted for these new uses by Francis Carter who had worked with Inigo Jones. The chapel was enlarged and the tower heightened with a bell turret and wooden cupola. A gallery was

The porch connecting the chapel and Master's Court. The walls are covered with memorials to famous former pupils. **Theo Bergström**

added to the Great Hall together with a new covered porch between the chapel and Master's Court. The fireplace in the Great Chamber was restored during Charles I's reign and emblazoned with his arms and initials. Sutton himself was buried in the chapel and in 1615 a fine monument was erected by Nicholas Stone; the marble carving is beautifully preserved and features Sutton's symbol, a greyhound's head.

The school flourished, acquiring an enviable reputation. All monarchs were on the Board of Governors and Oliver Cromwell attended several meetings. Joseph Addison and Richard Steele, the

An accurate 18th-century birdseye view of The Charterhouse. How easily this could be an Oxford or Cambridge college. **Finsbury Library**

dramatists and essayists, were contemporary scholars at the school, where they developed a life-long friendship. John Wesley was also a boy at Charterhouse from 1714–20.

Perhaps one of the most famous old boys was William Makepeace Thackeray, who was there between 1822 and 1828. During his school days he was "a gentle timid little fellow, who never cared to play games, and had no skill in them". For three years Thackeray was boarded out in Wilderness Row (now Clerkenwell Road) where he shared a room with Venables, the boy with whom he fought and who had his nose smitten flat. Not surprisingly he disliked school

intensely, and always referred to it as Slaughterhouse. The unpleasant memories faded in later years, and Charterhouse became his affectionate model for 'Greyfriars' in the *Newcomes*. He describes Sutton's tomb in the chapel:

"Its grotesque carvings, monsters, heraldries, darkles and shines with the most wonderful shadows and lights. There he lies, Fundator Noster, in his ruff and gown, awaiting the great Examination Day."

The hero of the book, Colonel Newcome, attended the school and ended his life there as a destitute old man. Thackeray himself attended an old boys' dinner only a few days before his death in 1863.

In the nineteenth century there were others who later made a name for themselves – Lord Baden-Powell of Mafeking and boy-scout fame, Viscount Fitzwilliam, who founded the Fitzwilliam Museum at Cambridge, and John Leech, the *Punch* artist.

By the mid-nineteenth century, however, the site was proving to be rather small for the expanding curriculum of the school, particularly with the Victorian fashion for sports and playing fields. In 1872, Charterhouse School moved to a large new site at Godalming, Surrey, where it continues to grow. It was replaced by Merchant Taylors', another school which moved there in 1873 from Upper Thames Street. Dr. Coggan, former Archbishop of Canterbury, was educated there, but in 1933 Merchant Taylors' also became too cramped and left for Rickmansworth, Hertfordshire.

St. Bartholomew's Medical School acquired most of the site – the playing fields, the headmaster's house, built in 1894, and Rutland Place, site of old Rutland House where William Davenant was allowed under the puritanical Cromwellian regime to produce his opera, *The Siege of Rhodes*. So Bart's finally reclaimed some of the 'No Man's Land' they had owned 600 years earlier.

One does not have to look too far for reminders of Charterhouse School. On the wooden refectory pillars generations of boys have carved their names or initials. Juvenile signatures are scratched on the original Elizabethan glass in the Great Chamber windows.

The hospice for old men has continued uninterrupted. The original criteria for admission in 1611 were that the pensioners or 'brothers' should be "decrepit or old Captaynes either at Sea or Land, Souldiers maymed or ympotent, decayed Marchaunts, men fallen into decaye through Shipwrecke Casualtie or Fyer or such evill Accident; those that have been Captives under the Turkes". The first 'brother', George Fenner, was a famous old Elizabethan sea captain, and over the years inmates have included some upstanding men who have fallen on hard times – Elkinah Settle, dramatist and rival of Dryden, Stephen Gray, pioneer of electricity, Tobias Hume, composer, and Alexander Macbean, assistant on Dr. Johnson's dictionary.

The conditions for entry are much the same today, except now the charity can only afford to support a maximum of forty. The pensioners must be British, over sixty, able-bodied men when admitted, and without any private income. Several of the gentlemen are in their nineties, and one occasionally sees them taking the air in Charterhouse Square. The Charterhouse still owns land north of Clerkenwell Road, part of Sutton's original endowment, from which it draws income to keep the charity going.

In May, 1941, The Charterhouse was badly gutted by incendiary bombs. A tremendous amount was lost irretrievably or badly damaged. The fine Elizabethan staircase on which Norfolk was arrested was completely destroyed. Over half the ceiling of the Great Chamber with its decorative painting was obliterated in the conflagration. Yet, amazingly, some good came from the devastation; during the restoration work, carried out by Seely and Paget, some fantastic discoveries shed new light on the history of The Charterhouse.

Until the havoc caused by the raid provided the chance for archaeologists to delve among the ruins, it had been assumed that the monastic chapel occupied the same site as the school chapel. Excavations in the floor of the Great Hall revealed the original line of the south limb of the cloisters, further south than had previously been supposed, suggesting that the monks' chapel may have also been further south and that the existing chapel would have been their chapter house. The clinching discovery came when a large chunk of

142 *The Great Elizabethan Chamber 1942. The ceiling and fireplace would appear to be damaged beyond repair.*
G.L.C.

The miraculous restoration, so well done that it is impossible to tell what is new and what original.
Theo Bergström

masonry fell away from the south wall of the tower to reveal a tapered hole or 'squint', clearly made to allow someone in the treasure chamber on the first floor to look down and watch something important below. Quite simply the squint enabled the monk standing guard to see the high altar and so participate in mass.

It had long been believed that Walter de Manny's body had been buried in 1372 at the foot of the high altar steps, according to his wish, as his tomb had never been found in the school chapel. Here, then, would be dramatic proof of the true location of the monastic church, and, sure enough, excavations unearthed a stone coffin containing a large lead coffin. On 20th May, 1947, the hermetically sealed coffin was opened amid hushed excitement, and there inside, incredibly well preserved, with a full head of bright red hair, was de Manny. Within seconds the body crumbled to dust under the strange atmospheric conditions; no-one had a camera. Beside the body was a lead disc or bulla, a gift from Pope Clement VI, 1342–52. The grave is now marked by an inscribed slab set in the lawn of the small garden between the chapel and Charterhouse Square. Where a fig tree now spreads its branches over the wall was de Manny's original hermitage chapel commemorating the plague victims.

The ruins of The Charterhouse were rebuilt phoenix-like from the ashes. The Elizabethan Great Chamber was superbly restored to its previous spendour. It is almost impossible to tell which is original and which post-war. A fine new oak staircase was built as a replacement, the banisters elegantly carved with Sutton's greyhounds, and the ugly Victorian stucco in Master's Court removed to reveal Lord North's stonework. The water conduit house was restored with its original pyramidal roof, and the Victorian buildings in Pensioners Court and Pump Court, with its ancient mulberry tree, were converted into flats and offices.

Today, The Charterhouse still conveys a vivid impression of a spacious Elizabethan country house, and contains a marvellous collection of treasures, such as the fifteenth-century oak table and stool in the lobby to the Great Hall, and the fine Flemish tapestries and English paintings of *The Last Supper* and *The Annunciation* on the fireplace surround in the Great Chamber. Royal governors are still entertained here – the Queen, Prince Philip and the Queen Mother in recent years. The Charterhouse remains very sequestered and quiet – a special appointment is required to be shown round. Traditions are closely guarded – even the leafy open space is private – but this undoubtedly preserves its enchanting tranquillity which contrasts so strikingly with the noise and bustle of the meat market, only a hundred yards away.

144 *The old Turnmill Street gin distillery facade, re-erected in Britton Street. Gin making is still a thriving local industry.* **Theo Bergström**

CHAPTER·5·
INDUSTRY & COMMERCE

While the meat market, Bartholomew's Hospital and the Post Office are the largest individual activities in the Smithfield area, there are also numerous other industrial and commercial enterprises. These include the meat and food trades, printing, textiles, jewellery and watches, as well as a whole host of miscellaneous businesses which exist here for no obvious locational reason. The mixture of different trades, of small and large firms, and of thriving and run-down businesses gives the Smithfield streets much of their character. About 8,000 people, almost as many as the market, hospital and Post Office put together, work in manufacturing or wholesaling in the area, and Smithfield remains one of Inner London's most important industrial centres. The proximity of Smithfield to the 'square mile' of the City and to the fashionable West End has also attracted many offices to the area. Although half of these relate to the local industries and commerce, there is a growing element of financial and professional city-orientated offices – now about 150 firms employing over 2,500 people.*

Smithfield's industrial tradition stretches back to the Middle Ages when craftsmen were attracted to the suburbs or 'liberties' to be free of the restrictive city guilds, or when obnoxious industries such as slaughtering, leather tanning, gluemaking and brickmaking were banned from inside the city walls. After the Great Fire in 1666, there was a further exodus from the city and in the nineteenth century industry in Smithfield and Clerkenwell consolidated and intensified, taking over many residential properties. During this period there was considerable commercial rebuilding, particularly north of the meat market, and a large number of miscellaneous activities set up in the area simply because of its convenience. Farmiloe's Glass and Royal Copenhagen Porcelain still exist in St. John Street although

*Tragically, industry is now, in 1990, an endangered species, as offices threaten to monopolize the area.

they are hardly typical Smithfield industries. This expansion was accompanied by a proliferation of service professions – shipping agents, banks, solicitors and brokers of every description.

Meat and food firms are the largest local industry despite the decline of recent years. Their link with the market is clearly vital, although many meat firms no longer depend on the market for supplies or customers as much as they used to. Some of the food and drink firms, especially brewers and distillers, settled here because of the good water supply. Booth's Gin distillery still flourishes on the corner of Clerkenwell Road and Turnmill Street.* The imposing art nouveau facade of the old distillery with its frieze depicting the five stages of gin-making, from ears of corn to tapping the barrel, has been re-erected in Britton Street. Many firms stay in the area because they are there, rather than for any modern locational tie.

Just as old as the meat trade is the clothing and textiles business. Originally this was based on the great medieval cloth fair, when Hosier Lane and Cloth Fair became the equivalents of Savile Row and Carnaby Street today. Mitchell, Inman and Co., at No. 40 Cloth Fair, is one of the few survivors; huge rolls of cloths and felts are stacked up above mahogany counters and shelves which have not changed since 1800.†

The London suburbs attracted Huguenot weavers, exiled from France in the seventeenth century; many settled in Spitalfields but some came to Smithfield and Clerkenwell, living and working in tiny garrets. Other trades related to clothing flourished in Smithfield. Leather manufacture thrived on the supply of hides from the cattle market; before modern synthetics, there was an unending demand

Mitchell, Inman and Co., Cloth Fair. **Theo Bergström**

BUTTONS

for leather shoes, bags, harnesses, saddles, book covers, parchments, etc. Buttons, fringes, millinery and fur traders also sprang up and prospered in the area. Most firms were very small, dependent on casual contacts with their neighbours and on local female labour. At the beginning of this century, Smithfield was at the heart of the cloth, millinery and fur trades.

These days are gone; since the war the clothing industry has shrunk to a dim shadow of its past, and looks likely to peter out altogether. Between 1972 and 1977 employment fell from 1,500 to 500, and the number of firms from 150 to 85. Bolton House, for example, built on a bomb site in Charterhouse Square in 1957, was occupied by Collet's the hat makers who employed 450 women; it closed in 1970.

Firms that remain find it increasingly difficult to find labour. War-time bombing and the drift of people out of Inner London have depleted the number of local workers; the rag trade now does best in the Greek Cypriot immigrant areas of Finsbury Park and Kentish Town. A few small firms struggle on, some having successfully carved a specialist niche in the West End fashion market. In Newbury Street there are still a couple of furriers, and even an ostrich feather merchant, while hand-stitched leather wallets and suitcases are made in St. John Street. There will always be an affluent society in London to buy their wares.

Printing came to Smithfield and Clerkenwell in a big way in the eighteenth century. In 1725, when Benjamin Franklin was a journeyman printer in Bartholomew Close, there were seventy-five master printers in London; by 1731 there were 124, and many of them

Reflections in an old shop window. Buttons were once made from hooves and horns. Now they are plastic, made in Hong Kong. **Theo Bergström**

147

located in the vicinity. Edward Cave at St. John's Gate is a notable case. Moreover, Smithfield has retained its locational advantages. In the early twentieth century there was a tremendous boom in popular newspapers and magazines, facilitated by cheap paper and new printing technology. This was concentrated in Fleet Street, but there were spin-offs for Smithfield. Specialists like plate-makers, type-setters, paper-creasers and lithographers needed to be near Fleet Street and the City, but not necessarily in expensive prestige premises. Even some newspapers have moved north – the *Daily Mirror* at Holborn Circus, and the *Morning Star* and the *Guardian* in Farringdon Road. Distribution firms such as Menzies have warehouses in the area, operating like the meat market in the early hours of the morning. Despite the unsuitability of some buildings for bulk handling and parking, the advantages of being close to customers has ensured that the printing and publishing trade in Smithfield is quite stable.

Another traditional activity more than holding its own is the craft jewellery and watch trade.* Clerkenwell has been the centre of the clock and watch industry since the eighteenth century. Two hundred years ago London clocks and watches were famed and sought after throughout the world for their elegance, reliability and supreme craftsmanship. By 1798 there were 7,000 artisans in Clerkenwell making or assembling watch parts; 60% of all watches were exported.

The north part of Smithfield, particularly along the Clerkenwell Road, is still littered with horological shops, makers and repairers. With the fad for 'digitalia' it is heartening to see specialist craftsmen

148   *St. John Street and Clerkenwell Road*
        are still the heart of the watch and
        clock trade. **Theo Bergström**

*They are less secure in 1990 as rocketing rents force people to move.

at work, like Mr. Parkes of Rowley and Parkes who repairs pendulum clocks in his lovely old workshop in Briset Street. Nothing here seems to have changed for centuries – the rickety wooden stairs, the dimly lit solid work bench, cluttered with a thousand cogs, an ordered jumble of dismantled time-pieces at different stages of repair. Nothing is hurried; customers happily wait for months, knowing the job will be well done.* Many craftsmen are symbiotic, relying heavily on their neighbours for different bits and pieces.

Smithfield is close to Hatton Garden, focus of the jewellery trade, and because rents are generally cheaper it has attracted a variety of dealers and craftsmen in precious metals. One of the most famous goldsmiths of modern times has his workshop and showroom at Nos. 90–92 St. John Street – Stuart Devlin, an Australian, who has enjoyed a meteoric career. Following his early triumph of winning the design for his country's decimal coinage, and a period in America and at the Royal College of Art, he settled in Smithfield in 1965, and has achieved world-wide recognition as the greatest living gold-smith, the man with the 'Midas touch'. His designs are contemporary and individual, but his methods are painstakingly traditional. His apprentices and master craftsmen undergo the most thorough train-ing; when a lad ends his five-year apprenticeship he is 'rung out' – all his fellow workers clang their tools together in a noisy ceremony to signify their acceptance of his new status.

Hand-raised goblets, cups and jugs, made from one sheet of metal, without any seams, are a speciality, and one of his craftsmen is the only spoon-maker left in the country. Many of Devlin's works are made on commission – special mementos, trophies and ornaments, like the exquisite set of silver nesting boxes made for the Prince of Wales as a gift to his parents on their silver wedding. A spirit of renaissance shines in his work – intrinsic beauty and craftsmanship for its own sake, rather than mass-produced functionalism. Encouragingly many of Devlin's assistants, who now number about fifty, are very young.

After a period in the doldrums, the Clerkenwell craft trades are once again flourishing – employment has almost doubled since 1970. The tremendous success of the Clerkenwell Workshops in Clerkenwell Close, a community of about 300 small craftsmen, is most heartening, and the demand for small, reasonably cheap premises is increasing. In many ways craft uses are ideally suited to the old buildings in Smithfield and Clerkenwell – small rooms, wooden floors, tight staircases and narrow streets are hopelessly impractical for modern large-scale ,heavy industry. The tiny quantities of raw materials and finished goods of the craftsmen do not pose loading problems – a month's supply of watches or jewels can fit in a suitcase. Security is a far more worrying hazard. Pennybank Chambers, a derelict tenement block on the corner of St. John's Square and

*Dan Parkes retired at the end of 1989, ending four generations of the family firm in Clerkenwell.

Clerkenwell Road, has been converted by Islington Council into small workshops; perhaps not the best or cheapest building to choose, but a laudable project if it succeeds.*

Amid so much decline in other traditional trades this, at least, gives some hope for the industrial future of the area. But the craft trades alone, whose employment is measured only in hundreds rather than thousands, are not a panacea. Undoubtedly industry in Smithfield has undergone a very bad patch in the last ten years.

150   *This photograph of St. John's Square looks older than 1946. Smith's continued to operate here until the mid-1980s. Now these buildings are smart offices.* **G.L.C.**

*Its success has exceeded expectation. If only it could have been a model for more.

Between 1972 and 1976 there was a 17% decline in manufacturing jobs and a 31% drop in occupied industrial floorspace. In 1972, only 8% of all industrial and commercial floorspace was empty, but by 1976 this figure had reached 27%. Clothing, meat and printing trades account for most of this. A cursory tour through the area reveals rows of estate agents' advertisement boards 'To Let' and 'For Sale', or barricaded windows and doorways, peeling paintwork and

fading signboards – 'Quality Sausage Casings', 'High Class Hats and Mantles', 'Fine Buttons and Trimmings', and a hundred other proud names from by-gone days. Newcomers are conspicuous, like the aerospace firm in Newbury Street or the occasional smart architect's or computer office.

The reasons for decline are multiple. As a rule, industry in Inner London has suffered not because the individual industries are particularly unhealthy from a national point of view (as is the case with the iron and steel or shipbuilding industries), but because the location is poor and uncompetitive. Smithfield, alas, has had the worst of both. Narrow streets and parking restrictions make loading and parking extremely difficult, while old buildings hinder mechanisation and may render expansion or modernisation impossible. A 10% survey of Smithfield firms revealed that 78% found parking and unloading a serious problem, while 70% complained of excessive rates and a poor environment for workers. Nearly half experience difficulties getting labour, especially skilled workers. This, of course, is a result of a far more alarming trend, the migration of the skilled worker from London seeking the cheap family house and garden to which he aspires and which London no longer offers. Once he has gone to a job at Stevenage or Basingstoke what is going to persuade him to spend £500 on an annual season ticket and three hours a day on a crowded train for the pleasure of working in Smithfield? Goverment incentives for industry to move to 'deprived areas', and on the negative side the time-consuming and bureaucratic rigmarole of obtaining Industrial Development Certificates in London, have not helped.

In Smithfield, moreover, there have been conservation constraints. While an old building may be unsuitable for modern machinery, neither is it desirable to pull it down and replace it with a single-storey pre-fabricated monstrosity. Albion Wire Works in Britton Street are a case in point, occupying an eighteenth-century house with narrow steep stairs, low ceilings and terribly cramped working conditions. The planners would never want to see the building destroyed, but are equally loath to see a non-industrial user move in. On the outside of the building is a wire model lion and unicorn made to be illuminated with gas jets for Queen Victoria's golden jubilee and restored for the silver jubilee in 1977. One wonders whether they will be there in 2002 A.D.*

Large empty buildings are a particular problem, like those north of the market in Charterhouse Street, Cowcross Street and St. John's Lane. Many of these commercial buildings, such as the purpose-built cold stores, need vast amounts of money to restore them, quite beyond the pocket of the normal small firm. More of the entrepreneurial efforts shown by Urban Small Space at Clerkenwell Workshops and by Islington Council at Pennybank Chambers are urgently required

*They had gone by 1982!

so that the manufacturer can move into ready-converted units, paying reasonable rents. The longer a building stands empty the more it deteriorates and the more expensive it becomes to restore; meanwhile, pressure mounts for demolition or for allowing a more lucrative office use to pay for it.

Islington Council has taken a firm stance in support of industry,* discouraging other uses. This is to some extent justifiable on employment grounds — 28% of workers in industry and commerce in Smithfield live in Inner London, compared with only 8% of office workers. Clearly industry provides more local jobs, and could help to reduce the already high level of local unemployment. Furthermore, in the last couple of years, there does seem to have been an industrial revival, or at least a levelling off of decline, north of the meat market. Out of 43,000 square metres of industrial and commercial floorspace vacant in 1975, 17,500 square metres had been let by 1977, and only a further 5,500 square metres had become empty. The implementation of industrial planning permissions in 1975–6 was twice that of the previous two years. South of the market, where the Corporation of London has been more lenient in allowing industrial buildings to change to other uses, the amount of empty industrial and commercial premises continues to increase. The 'hope-value' of obtaining permission for office development stifles any incentive to relet an empty building for an industrial use.

Regrettably it seems inevitable that the old fabric and poor access will continue to cause firms to leave or close down. Already there has been a marked change in the nature of activities, with a take-over by administration at the expense of manufacturing. In 1976 only 35% of workers in so-called manufacturing or wholesaling firms were actually 'operatives', while 45% were office or sales staff. Of course, none of this is unique to Smithfield, but in such a traditional area the change has perhaps been more sudden and damaging to the character of the place.

Existing planning control over land use changes is negative and slow-working. What is required is a positive stimulus to local industry, by improving parking and loading arrangements or allocating grants and loans on the lines of an Industrial Improvement Area, such as the Rochdale experiment. A careful blend of private enterprise with discreet and selective Government help is surely the only way of keeping and encouraging industry and commerce in Smithfield and so preserving the jobs of thousands of Londoners.

*The changes in the planning law now relegate this text to academic and historic interest.

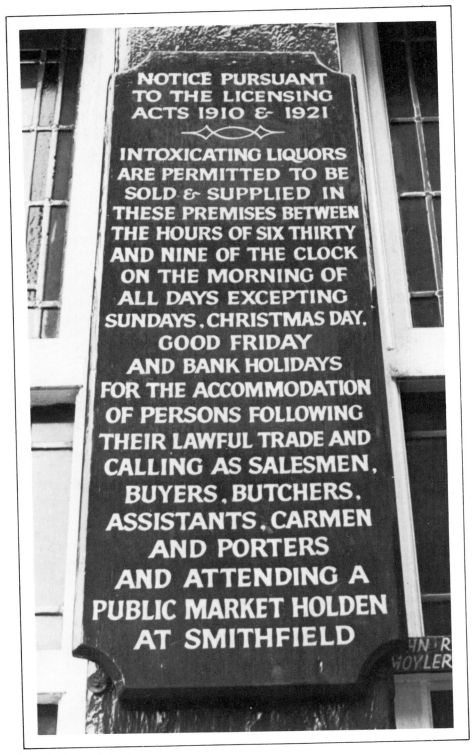

154   *The Smithfield Tavern.*
       Theo Bergström

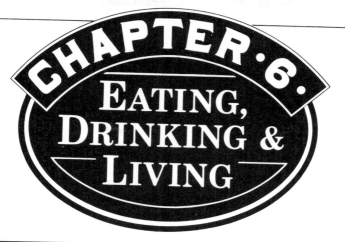

PUBLIC HOUSES

Smithfield has such a large number of pubs that it would take even the most enthusiastic drinker a good while to explore them all. The variety and character of pubs reveal much about an area, for they are the watering holes for the people who live and work in the area, without whom nothing would exist.

In previous centuries, when Smithfield was more prosperous* and thousands of residents and businesses crammed into the congested streets, there were correspondingly more pubs. People also drank more; before tea and coffee arrived, ale was the daily beverage for all who could not afford wine. Best ale was 1d a gallon in 1300, and most people would drink a gallon a day. Habits die hard for some! The heyday of the pub was the nineteenth-century, when the tax on beer was reduced to discourage spirit drinking. In 1830, a justice's licence was no longer required to open a beer house and despite the temperance movement and the introduction of licensing hours, pubs proliferated. A map of 1885 shows seventy pubs in the area bounded by Clerkenwell Road, Goswell Road, Farringdon Road and Newgate Street, and this is after many had been demolished for new roads and railways in the 1850s. There were twenty-three pubs in St. John Street alone.

Most of the really famous Smithfield pubs have unfortunately disappeared completely – the Old Jerusalem Tavern in St. John's Gate, renowned for its pineapple rum and cordial gin, and a short distance down St. John's Lane the Old Baptist's Head where chained prisoners travelling from Clerkenwell to Newgate could pause and slurp down a mind-dulling cup of ale. This pub, with its fine, painted sign of John the Baptist's head on a charger, was originally part of an Elizabethan house, and when pulled down in 1898 its fireplace was removed to St. John's Gate. South of the cattle market the Fortune of

*Prosperity, though not population,
have now returned.

155

War at Pye Corner was the haunt of bodysnatchers while the Bull and Mouth Inn in St. Martin's-le-Grand was one of London's finest coaching inns. Goswell Road and Aldersgate Street were lined with inns and taverns serving the coaching station at St. Martin's – the Old White Hart, Brown Bear, Old Parr's Head, Red Lion, Horse and Crown, Half Moon, Swan and Horse Shoe, Rose and Crown, and many more. The demise of the coach trade was their death also. Some of the alleys leading off Aldersgate are remnants of old tavern yards – Half Moon Passage, Glasshouse Yard and Cross Keys Square.

Many other pubs served the cattle and meat markets – the Red

156 *The Old Dick Whittington stood on the corner of Middle Street and Cloth Fair until 1913. Ye Olde Red Cow behind survives.* **Museum of London**

Cow, the Cow and Gate, the Smithfield Tavern and the New Market (with a ludicrous modern sign showing a racehorse). Most of these have unusual opening hours to cater for the early morning workers, 6.30 a.m. to 9.30 a.m. It used to be earlier; in the market itself the Cock Tavern once opened at 4.00 a.m. serving its speciality, 'wazzer', a bracing concoction of hot tea laced with whisky, fit to warm the coldest cockles.

With the steady decline in traditional Smithfield activities, it is hardly surprising that several pubs have closed since the war. The Rising Sun at No. 38 Cloth Fair, beside Rising Sun Court, and the Globe at the bottom end of Hosier Lane are still standing but have been empty for years. More recently, the White Horse in Little Britain closed, blighted by unnecessary redevelopment proposals. This was a charming old place, with painted tiles, polished wood panelling and a delightful archway through into Cross Keys Square. How pleasing it would be to see these bars pulling pints of beer again one day.

Of the remaining twenty or so pubs we can be thankful that there is still a wide selection to choose from, satisfying most tastes. For the benefit of the real ale drinker they are easily divisible into two categories, but some are more pleasant or interesting than others. Moreover, nothing is constant; a good pub can be ruined overnight by the whims of a new landlord or the insensitivity of brewery managers. The Bishop's Finger in West Smithfield is an example. Since the departure of the old landlord, with his magnificent handle-bar whiskers, twinkling eyes, ample girth and *basso profundo*, as often as not mixing with the customers, the charm of the place has gone, at least for me. Although the Shepherd Neame beer is still excellent (the best pint for many a mile) there is now a plush new carpet sprawling

The Rising Sun in 1980, happily now risen again, thanks to Sam Smith's.
Theo Bergström

157

remorselessly over the old saw-dust floor and a slick food bar; such is the brewer's concept of progress. The bar gets too full of pin-stripes at lunch-time.

Perhaps the most genuine pub is the Castle in Cowcross Street next to Farringdon Station, with well kept I.P.A. and a meat market

158 *Lunchtime at the Castle. The painting depicts George IV pawning his watch at the bar to pay his gambling debts.* **Theo Bergström**

clientele. A pawnbroker's sign hanging in the bar commemorates an unscheduled visit by George IV. In keeping with his extravagant, rakish ways he had gambled all his money at a local cockfight and, to raise more funds, pawned his watch at the bar. As a reward, he granted the landlord a pawnbroker's licence which his present-day

The Hope, Cowcross Street, just across from the market. **Theo Bergström**

successor, a cheerful Irishman, still holds.

The Sutton Arms in Carthusian Street is also a pleasant pub, with a fine glass barrel-like bow front. The unpretentious saloon is usually crowded with jolly medics supping draught Bass or I.P.A. The Viaduct Tavern on the corner of Giltspur Street and Newgate Street, serving Ind Coope Burton, is a genuine Victorian 'gin palace', with a high, elaborately-moulded ceiling, cut-glass, painted mirrors and plush seats, usually full of off-duty (one hopes) postmen. None of the other real beer pubs are particularly distinguished. The Barley Mow, sandwiched between Long Lane and Cloth Fair, was reputedly one of Lord Lucan's haunts, and like the White Hart in Giltspur Street does smart upstairs business lunches. The White Bear in St. John Street has no frills.

A number of other pubs in the area are worth a visit for their atmosphere and character, if not for their beer. The Hand and Shears on the corner of Kinghorn and Middle Streets was where the tailors used annually to elect their chairman. The cosy interior, with low ceiling, hard floors and wood panelling, ensures its popularity. The Fox and Anchor at No. 115 Charterhouse Street has a very fine architectural exterior, with glazed terracotta and painted decorative tiles showing strong art nouveau influence. The oak framed doorway and mullioned and transomed leaded windows verge on the mock Jacobean. Inside, the long thin bar has a real chophouse flavour with friendly barmaids serving excellent greasy breakfasts. The Hope in Cowcross Street also has a splendidly ornate facade, with two doors either side of a central elliptically-arched bow window with decorated glass spandrels. The Smithfield Tavern, virtually next door to the Fox and Anchor and with a thriving early morning trade, has cows' heads surmounting the pediments beside the door.

Too many pubs have been ruined in recent years by senseless modernization and standardization. The new Coach and Horses in St. John Square is completely soulless. Even the quaint old signboard, which showed the Exeter mail coach being attacked by an escaped lioness on the open road near Salisbury in October, 1816, has been removed. How boring.

SHOPS AND CAFES

The commercial boom in the nineteenth century saw a mushrooming of eating houses to provide the hundreds of clerks with their cooked lunch at one o'clock. Dining and chop houses abounded, a few of which survive, almost unaltered, like the Bartholomew Restaurant near the hospital, with its clean linen table cloths, respectable wooden chairs and plain English menu. The Charterhouse Grill in Charterhouse Square has moved with the times and changed into a rather exclusive steak house, catering for city gents on expense accounts.

Today there is a host of tiny snack bars around the market where market workers lounge over formica tables and wolf down door-step sandwiches and stewed tea. Still, they are cheap. Most seem to be run by Italians, like Mrs. Bartholdi who has been in Smithfield since the war. A couple of new smart restaurants, like the Cowcross, feed the executives and managers. All the custom is lunchtime and weekday; hardly anywhere is open in the evenings or at weekends.

Most of the shops in the area similarly cater for lunchtime house-wives or browsers, cigarette smokers and newspaper readers, but there are a few pleasant exceptions. The window of Denny's bookshop in Carthusian Street is dominated by medical tomes, while Fuller-scopes in Farringdon Road has been making brass telescopes there for 150 years and sell everything the amateur astronomer could want. Gedges* in St. John Street is a delightfully old-fashioned Vic-torian shop, with scrubbed wooden counters, selling paints and creo-sotes, and Mitchell Inman in Cloth Fair sell their cloth just as they did 100 years ago. The antique dealer in Cloth Fair and the numisma-tic shop in St. John Street are perhaps the first of more tourist trades to come.

General shopping is rather limited – Gamages at Holborn Circus was the last City department store, demolished several years ago – but the carnivore is well cared for at Hart's Corner and other butchers near the market who retail Smithfield meat and poultry. Dufaire's and Links† in Cowcross Street sell a fine range of whole cheeses. For fruit and veg. the street markets of Leather Lane and White Cross Street are not too far away.

One of the area's curiosities is the Farringdon Road book market. This was started by a Mr. James Dabbs shortly after the opening of the Holborn Viaduct and quickly became a mecca for cheap second-hand book enthusiasts. Maybe Dabbs was attracted by the historical literary associations nearby; within a stone's throw are Richard Savage's birth place, Charles Lamb's school, Johnson's and Gold-smith's houses and the place where Chatterton, the wondrous boy poet, came to his untimely end. The setting has now been ruined by the traffic thundering down Farringdon Road, and has become an awkward and unpleasant place for those who wish to browse among this tatterdemalion market of the unwanted. Graham Greene was struck by the place:

"A sunk railway track and a gin distillery flank the gritty street. There is something Victorian about the whole place – an air of ugly commercial endeavour mixed with old idealism and philanthropies. It isn't only the jumble of unattractive titles on the dusty spines, the huge weight of morality at sixpence a time, even the setting has an earnestness. . . . The public houses are

* Now Hutchinson's, but otherwise mercifully unchanged.
† Moved to a Waterloo railway arch in 1986.

161

162 *The back alleys of Cloth Fair, 1877;
truly medieval houses which new
public health legislation was soon to
sweep away.* **G.L.C.**

like a lesson in temperance."

Certainly it now takes a frequent visitor to appreciate the faint charm of the place.

RESIDENTS

It is hard to believe that Smithfield was once one of London's most densely populated residential areas. Today, at the end of the working day and at weekends, the streets are quiet and deserted – the territory of cats and caretakers. Yet at one time, when it was normal for most people to walk to work, many actually lived over their place of work – there was often no alternative, for the poor at least. Until cleared away in the 1840s, the rookeries of the Fleet valley were notoriously overcrowded and squalid, although in the eighteenth century other parts of Smithfield such as Britton Street, Charterhouse Square and St. John's Square had been fashionable Georgian residences.

Population levels in Clerkenwell Ward reached a peak in the 1861 census when there were 65,000 residents. During the mid-nineteenth century Briset Street, Albion Place and Benjamin Street were lined with mean artisans' terraces. Ragged schools, parochial schools and boarding schools sprang up; Dominion House in Bartholomew Close, built by Aston Webb in 1878, was originally a boarding school, while the old school in Eagle Court has been taken over by Smithfield Meat College. There was also a school in Lamb and Flag Court now obliterated by Booth's distillery. Smithfield was a place where people were born, lived and died. In the crowded back alleys children played in the street:

"Most families were large and the children used to play many collective games, such as cops and robbers, hop scotch, hide and seek, besides the seasonal games such as hoops, four-stones, shuttlecock, tops, tip-cat." *A Smithfield childhood 1896–1906*

The worst of the slums were gradually swept away by the zealous Victorian reformers, and with the advent of the railways and a new era of cheap public transport people began to leave Inner London for the new suburbs which sprawled out into the surrounding countryside. The exodus was irrevocable; in 1887 St. Andrew's, Holborn, regularly had a congregation of 900 on a Sunday, but by 1902 there were only 400. Today there are no Sunday services and the church is locked at weekends.

Many of the residents who were evacuated in 1939 never returned. Sadly, population has continued to dwindle since the war, and today by far the majority of residents are hospital staff, mainly nurses, living in hostels such as Gloucester House nurses' home or in the flats at Nos. 6–9 Charterhouse Square, an elegant 1930s block with the

'latest' curved glass windows. Most private residents are landlords living over pubs, shopkeepers, caretakers, or attached to the Charterhouse. In 1961 there were still 600 private residents living in the area bordered by Clerkenwell Road, Farringdon Road, Newgate Street and Aldersgate/Goswell Road: by 1976 there were 350. How many will there be in 1991? Mrs. Dallanegra who lived at No. 16 Briset Street all her life was one of Smithfield's last born and bred; she died in 1977, in her nineties, taking her childhood memories with her.

Smithfield is no longer a very suitable area for children or old people. The streets are busy with dangerous traffic, while there is very little open space and none where a child could enjoy a good game

164   *Bartholomew Close, 1880. The novelty*
of the camera clearly shows. Hogarth
was born here in 1697.   **G.L.C.**

Aylesbury Place, one of Smithfield's slums, in 1906. The tattered bill on the left spells imminent demolition. **G.L.C.**

Mallory Buildings replaced it, a model dwelling for its time. The tram tracks and cobbles are now buried under tarmac in St. John Street. **G.L.C.**

165

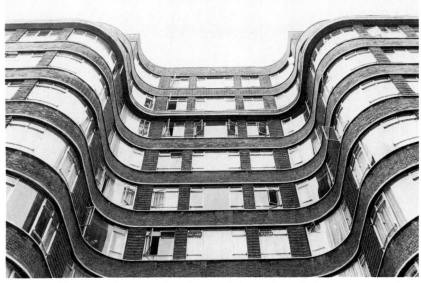

of football or cowboys and indians. The noise of the meat market, particularly the incessant roar and rumble of lorries' refrigeration engines on summer nights has exasperated residents trying to sleep or watch television. Sir John Betjeman, every inch a Londoner, used to live at No. 43 Cloth Fair until the hellish noise of European articulated lorries drove him out.

Despite this, Sir John loved the unique atmosphere of the area – the weekend tranquillity, the narrow alleys and passages, the cheery Chaucerian Smithfield workers. Too many people who know only the rush hour are over-eager to write off the City as a place to live, obsessed as they are with pre-conceived notions. If one knows where to look, there are tennis courts, bowling greens and swimming pools, and the Finsbury Leisure Centre all within a short walk. So, too, are the Sunday morning markets at Petticoat Lane and Brick Lane. How many commuters have seen kestrels or herons over London Wall, or heard the evening peal of St. Bartholomew's?

The Golden Lane estate on the east side of Goswell Road, designed by Chamberlin, Powell and Bon in 1953–62 has helped to keep some vitality in the area. The Barbican was planned to do the same, but the high rents have meant that many Barbican residents own second homes or weekend retreats which rather defeats the object. Despicably, the City Corporation has even considered letting empty flats as offices. One really wonders at the original intentions.

Any substantial increase in the Smithfield population is likely to be through the efforts of St. Bartholomew's Hospital which desperately needs more accommodation for nurses, junior medical staff and doctors who are 'on call'. There is also scope for small private residential developments, even if they can only be financed as part of mixed commercial schemes. Two such schemes have been proposed in Charterhouse Square, which is most welcome. With escalating public transport costs, the advantages of walking or cycling to work would attract many people if the accommodation was available. Given the growth in the local craft trades, there must be a market for combined studio/residential units where the craftsman can live above his workshop.

It is vital that the local authorities take a positive step to encourage this. Islington Council has done little in the past to help the Smithfield area, perhaps understandably when it has more pressing housing problems elsewhere. However, they did oppose the Yorke, Rosenberg and Mardall development in Britton Street which included offices, workshops and flats and the reconstruction of the distillery facade; fortunately the Secretary of State upheld the appeal. Judging from the 1978 Smithfield Area Plan, Islington is now taking a more enlightened attitude and attempted to acquire the Britton Street flats for key local workers. On the City side there are opportunities for small-scale housing schemes on the derelict sites of Nos. 26–37 Cloth Fair and No. 73 Long Lane which have been owned by the Corporation's Planning Committee for years. Here is a marvellous chance to provide a dozen houses or flats at present needlessly going to waste.

Flats or maisonettes could well solve the problem of unwanted upper floors in older buildings where workshops or offices could occupy the more accessible and viable ground floors. Too often in the past office blocks have been allowed with one or two penthouse flats perched on top. These merely serve as a managing director's last resort if he misses the last train to Esher, or in time are converted to offices. They do nothing to bring full-time residents back to Smithfield.

With some justification the residents consider themselves to be a hard-done-by minority. Tubes and buses stop running early and pubs and shops shut at evenings and weekends. The local councils could do something towards improving living conditions. Islington has introduced a night-time lorry parking ban on its streets, but it really must persuade the police to enforce the restriction if it is to have any effect, and should equip the lorry park with the facilities necessary to make drivers want to use it. A few more residents' parking bays and the abolition of Saturday morning parking restrictions would also be a welcome gesture.

In the long term, however, a real improvement will only come if more people are living in the area. Publicans and shopkeepers will then find it worth their while to open longer hours, and a vociferous local community will be able to press for the local services which they expect from their rates.

168 *Christchurch, Newgate Street   the*
superb Wren tower and ruined nave.
Theo Bergström

CHAPTER·7·
PLANNING FOR THE FUTURE

As has been seen, Smithfield contains a wide range of activities and institutions; some are declining, others remain stable, and a few are expanding. Change is inevitable in any area; nowhere can become fossilized, unless it is destined to be a museum. Indeed, evolution is essential for survival. The 64,000 dollar question today is how much control should be exercised in the name of the 'common good' to restrict the purely economic forces of the free market. Such control, for good or ill, is largely left to the town planners, and the elected politicians who are their masters.

In 1976 Islington Council and the City Corporation, adjacent local authorities but with opposing political colours, commendably decided to join forces in a plan for the Smithfield area. Here was a clearly identifiable local area with common problems, where the local authority boundary was a meaningless divide. (Why the old city boundary was not rationalized to follow Charterhouse Street and Carthusian Street in 1866, or in 1965 when London Boroughs were re-organized, Heaven knows! Instead it still wriggles aimlessly along the lines of long forgotten back alleys and yards and actually cuts through several buildings whose occupants have to pay rates to both councils!)

Unhappily, the Smithfield Area Plan – despite its good intentions and brave words – has done little more than identify the problems and has only partially shown how the revitalization of this decaying area might be achieved. Smithfield is an outstanding example of the difficulties of conservation in an old urban area; this is conservation in its broadest sense, not just the preservation of old buildings but the maintenance of traditional activities, jobs and the historic character of the area. Different conservation objectives conflict and place the unfortunate planner in a series of awkward dilemmas. The Smithfield Area Plan has succeeded in highlighting the choices but has only gone a little way to resolving them or suggesting priorities.

LAND USE

L and use remains the basis of planning, if only because it is the physical expression of wider social and environmental issues which planners like to think they deal with. In Smithfield, the future of the meat market is a central land use issue which the City Corporation has failed to face up to squarely. The traditional Smithfield site may not be the most efficient or profitable location for a large wholesale market, but its survival is crucial to the character and employment of the area. Although the decline in the associated meat trades has been worrying, it is nothing to the mass exodus that would follow the market's closure. While it now seems highly improbable that the Greater London Council* will interfere and do a 'Covent Garden' at Smithfield, no-one has seriously investigated the feasibility of other uses such as transferring Billingsgate fish market or a weekend market to fill some of Smithfield's vacant space should the meat market continue to contract. The two original meat market buildings are extremely important architecturally; their demolition and redevelopment would be unthinkable.

Another key land use problem revolves around the future of traditional industry in the area and the alternative pressures for office development. Administrative functions have been creeping into and replacing industrial operations within existing Smithfield firms, but in addition independent offices have increased in the area, some related to or serving the area like solicitors and brokers but many more alien to the area. Smithfield is a cheap convenient location, close enough to both the City and the West End to attract a large number of businesses who need to be fairly central, but cannot or do not wish to pay the extravagant rents of Piccadilly or Cheapside. Employment in 'city and professional' offices increased by about 25% between 1972 and 1976. Should further office development be allowed in Smithfield or would the area be better off without?

The dangers of flinging open the doors to offices are palpable. Offices are profitable and can afford to pay higher rents or buy land at a higher price than any other private land use. Moreover since the war, central London has become the main office centre in the country – everybody wants to be there, the demand for accommodation has until recently been insatiable, which in turn has forced up rents and land values. Traditional Smithfield uses – industry, commerce, shops, pubs and cafes and even older local offices – simply could not compete in a free market.

*The GLC was abolished in 1986.

A large amount of land in the Smithfield area is owned by large institutions such as St. Bartholomew's Hospital, The Charterhouse or insurance companies. Where they are not using the land for their own purposes it is held as an investment. If the institution relies on the income received, there has to be a strong sentimental reason for not trying to maximise the rent. With no planning control, industrial and commercial firms might be forced out when their leases expire, or bought out by financial offers they would find hard to refuse. Traditional industrial, commercial, retail, residential and service trades would be lost irretrievably.

From the employment aspect alone this would be a bad thing, putting many local people out of work. From a wider angle it would be disastrous for the overall character and flavour of the area. Smithfield's charm lies in its variety and juxtaposition of different activities. To allow Smithfield to become part of a huge amorphous, homogeneous office zone would be inexcusable.

Islington Council have tried to take a tough line against office developments on the north side of the market and have been supported by the Greater London Council, who similarly do not consider the area as a preferred location for offices. Some of the pressure for office development is speculative, that is where a developer buys land cheaply, obtains permission for a new use and sells at a profit – easy money even after development tax. It is felt that this pressure has already caused some of the industrial decline in Smithfield. Loss of actual or potential industrial employment has been the main ideological reason for refusing permission for offices. As was suggested in Chapter five, Islington Council may point to the recent industrial revival and claim that their approach has been justified. On the City side where offices have been given virtual *carte blanche*, the industrial decline has been almost total. Some of the last remaining industrial buildings in Newbury Street and Middle Street are now threatened by office redevelopment for a City livery company.

All this has not been without problems, however, as displayed by the multitude of empty buildings and derelict sites apparently unwanted by industry or commerce. Planners only have negative powers in that they cannot prevent redundancies or a firm closing down, and once an industrial building is empty they can only stop or allow a non-industrial use. There are no controls over implementation.

Surely the answer for the Smithfield area on both sides of the market is moderation – a carefully controlled policy allowing some office development on a limited basis. Several buildings in the area are so dilapidated that only some office element will produce enough rent to pay for their restoration. Other buildings may be unsuitable in size, layout, structure or access for total industrial use, and offices, say on the upper floors, may be the only viable means of getting the whole building back into use. The acceptance of mixed use is the key and demands a flexibility based on the merits and qualities of each individual building. Treated as a subsidising element offices may be a convenient method of providing more desirable uses such as light industry, craft workshops and housing. This concept of 'planning gain' is one that Islington recognises, but perhaps in the past has held out for too much; if the profit incentive is whittled down too far developers will look elsewhere.

Offices have some things in their favour. They do not clutter the streets with vans and lorries or aggravate traffic congestion, and while offices themselves may not employ many inner London residents, they help to support local service trades, shops and cafes. Preference could be given to small office units; these are more likely to be professional firms who have always had a place in Smithfield – small firms who cannot afford the ridiculous city rents or who cannot find a small enough office in the enormous city blocks. The City Corporation have imposed a 12,000 square feet maximum per unit in Smithfield, but this is hardly small – 3,000 square feet would be more realistic. In the five years between 1972 and 1976, Islington Council refused nineteen office applications in the Smithfield area. Although an equal number got through some of these were upheld on appeal, and most of the others were small developments, under 4,000 square feet; 86% of permissions were implemented, which is encouraging.

Offices are not a panacea, but under certain circumstances they may help to attract investment back into Smithfield. There is no reason why a sensible approach to offices should conflict with a policy to protect and encourage traditional Smithfield uses or with support for new hospital and residential accommodation. The high land costs will preclude private housing in Smithfield unless it is part of a mixed scheme, or built by a large institution such as the hospital, medical school or City University, which should all be encouraged to provide more flats or hostels. The newly completed shops, offices and flats on the old bomb site at Nos. 80–83 Long Lane is just the sort of small-scale mixed scheme which should be welcomed and encouraged.

DERELICTION AND BLIGHT

Investment is desperately needed in the Smithfield area. Since the war so much has declined – the market, manufacturing, commerce, local population, schools, shops and pubs. Vacant and derelict sites have proliferated – forgotten bomb sites in Cloth Fair, unwanted railway buildings along Farringdon Road, defunct cold stores, and cleared ground either awaiting the developer's magic wand or used temporarily (though seemingly indefinitely) for car parking. Despite the plethora of official bureaucratic reasons and excuses, the combination paints a depressing picture of waste land, decrepit buildings, eyesores, hoardings and corrugated iron. As well as degrading the appearance of the streets it inhibits any economic confidence in the area. The rows of 'To Let' boards must put off some people; who wants to sail in a sinking ship?

Empty buildings and vacant sites moreover are a potentially wasted opportunity for employment or housing, and a loss in rate income to the council. The temporary car parks at the bottom of St. John Street or in Hosier Lane only delay permanent development of these empty sites, producing a tidy income for the owners and for National Car Parks in the meantime. Parking, if needed, should be included as part of mixed developments. It has been repeatedly argued that greater penalties against owners of empty sites and buildings should be imposed through the rate system. This might dissuade owners from deliberately keeping buildings empty in the hope of getting an office permission if they wait long enough. It is about time something was done instead of so much idle chatter.

Sadly, the Corporation of London itself is one of the main culprits. Some of the old bomb sites south of the market have been neglected simply through apathy (at least the land might have been sold or leased to a housing association). Far worse, however, the Corporation is responsible for the concentration of derelict properties in the Little Britain/Cox's Court area, which have been systematically purchased and prematurely emptied in advance of a new road planned to carve through the area.

The proposal is part of Route 11, a grandiose scheme first conceived in the 1947 post-war plan for the reconstruction of the devastated city which included a northern by-pass skirting the city. The first section was built in the 1960s between Aldersgate Street and Moorgate in an area that had been completely flattened by bombing – a wide dual carriageway road with separate overhead pedestrian walkways, and flanked by enormous slab-like office blocks. This is London Wall, though it neither follows the wall nor the line of the original street of that name. The original proposal was to extend this major road artery westwards to link up with Holborn Viaduct and Newgate Street, cutting through the Little Britain area which was not badly damaged in the war.

Surprisingly, the plan has its eminent supporters. Sir Nikolaus Pevsner acclaimed the new London Wall development with enthusiasm:

> "It promises to be of high aesthetic value and London's most advanced concept of central area development. Execution has begun and is making good progress."

> "The only great pity is that the whole of London Wall is so short. No sooner have you stepped on the gas than you have to

brake because you have reached the Aldersgate end . . . . To walk around London Wall is a pleasure. The railings are of metal and look light – so do the buildings – the very opposite of the new buildings and the upper walks by the Hayward Gallery and the Purcell and Queen Elizabeth Halls. . . . 1960 certainly is more attractive than 1970."

Well, fashions change and future generations will make their own judgements.

The Little Britain scheme is an outrageous example of the worst effects of planning blight and the dogmatic pursuit of an outdated master plan no longer justified by present day circumstances. Damage to the area has already been serious, although the old buildings fronting Little Britain and facing Postman's Park still form a delight-

174   *London Wall, 1960, an area
       devastated by German bombing. The
       ideals of 1950s planning are taking
       shape – a dual carriageway and
       massive tower blocks.* **G.L.C.**

*Twenty years later the new London
Wall is complete. The Museum is
surrounded by a sea of office blocks.*
Theo Bergström

ful group. Little Britain is where Jaggers had his office in *Great Expectations* – "just out of Smithfield and close by the coach office – a gloomy street where dust and grit lay thick on everything." No. 12, built in 1858, is a fine warehouse with columns and arcaded windows, while No. 22 has a rare Georgian shopfront, sadly neglected and decayed. The disused White Horse pub has a lovely tiled arch which leads through to Cross Keys Square and more dilapidation. Cox's Court, Montague Court, Westmorland Buildings and Albion Buildings are also under the axe. A few businesses, like the City Recorder, struggle on in modest upstairs rooms, but the City Corporation surveyor will only allow very short leases which discourages any initiative.

South of Little Britain, the peace of Postman's Park and the setting of St. Botolph's, Aldersgate, one of London's quietest oases, would be shattered by the new road, and all for no reason. Traffic levels along London Wall are incredibly low for the size of the road. The existing one-way system round Angel Street, King Edward Street, Newgate Street and St. Martin's, is more than adequate even in rush hour.

Seemingly nothing will change the minds of the city authorities now. Unbelievably, the new road is regarded as a planning benefit and will therefore be accompanied by a massive office development to pay for it. In November, 1977, a planning application was submitted by Jafton Properties Ltd. (development agents for the City) and St. Bartholomew's Hospital for 383,500 square feet of offices and 124,000 square feet of housing (for the hospital). The hostel accommodation is welcome, but could surely be provided in a more satisfactory way. All the buildings in Little Britain could be rehabilitated for workshops, small offices and flats while the area towards Bartholomew Close could accommodate small scale high density housing for the hospital, based on the existing street pattern.

Instead it seems only a matter of time before the financial i's are dotted and t's crossed and development starts. The network of historic courts and alleys and the jumble of old buildings will be swept away and obliterated for ever. Meanwhile, the truncated ends of elevated walkways stand at the Aldersgate end of London Wall, waiting to be continued westwards. Once begun, where will these high level pavements end? Man is a ground-level animal; if God had meant man to fly . . . .

The Corporation's ruthlessness has already been seen in their treatment of Wren's Christchurch, burnt out in the war. In 1974 the fine east end and south side wall which had survived intact were demolished for road widening. Now only the north wall and west end with its elegant tower remain, while the nave is open to the roar of passing traffic. Here was a marvellous opportunity for preserving a memorial to the blitz, like the gutted Coventry cathedral, with a sheltered garden in the nave. An extra few feet of road and a wider kerb radius were considered more important.

CONSERVATION AND DESIGN

The Little Britain case is just an example of the need for a strong conservation policy throughout the area. This must involve the protection of historic street lines, rehabilitation of old buildings, and the insistence on high standards of design in new buildings, so that they complement rather than detract from the appearance of the area. Enormous damage has already been done, in the Cock Lane/Hosier Lane area for example. The character of these narrow, shadowy, cobbled streets has been ruined by large new buildings, set back from the old street frontage, and by vast expanses of car parking. One of the last old houses on the north side of Cock Lane was demolished recently. Through the peeling stucco and giant wooden props one could decipher the name on the shop front – 'Lidstone, founded 1843'. They departed long ago; now their building is gone and with it another link with the past. North of the market a proposal to widen Briset Street, demolishing the workshop of Rowley and Parkes the clock repairers, would be a further incursion into the medieval pattern of lanes.

The historic and architectural character of the area has been acknowledged to some extent by the designation of 'conservation areas', which among other things brings the demolition of all buildings under planning control. North of the market most of the area up to Clerkenwell is protected, but to the south only St. Bartholomew's precinct, Cloth Fair and West Smithfield are included. Postman's

176 *How long before the walkway*
    continues its march of destruction?
    Ahead lies Little Britain, Postman's
    Park and St. Botolph's.
    Theo Bergström

Park, Little Britain and St. Botolph's and Snow Hill/St. Sepulchre's should be designated as two further conservation areas before it is too late.

Many important individual or groups of buildings are listed by the Department of the Environment for their special architectural or historic interest, and so protected from demolition or alteration. Nearly all the eighteenth century or earlier buildings in Smithfield are statutorily listed, but there are many nineteenth and early twentieth century buildings of special interest that are not listed at present. Some of the decorative commercial buildings in St. John Street, Cowcross Street, Charterhouse Street and Little Britain are examples of a lavish style of Victorian building now rare in central London. The facade of Farringdon Metropolitan Railway station, with its cream faience tiles, is also worth protecting for its historical value. Islington Council is pressing the D.O.E. to extend its listing, and has established a 'local list' of buildings of individual or street value, which though not protected by law, advertises the council's concern. The City Corporation has not asked the D.O.E. to list more buildings, nor have they ever shown much enthusiasm in serving building preservation notices when an important non-listed building is threatened.

The maintenance and restoration of listed buildings should be a high priority. Where a listed building is in poor condition, any use or combination of uses which will achieve its full rehabilitation should be encouraged. The imposition of V.A.T. on repair and maintenance, but not on brand new building, is an absurd differentiation and handicap.

Farringdon Station, Cowcross Street;
the original terminus of the
Metropolitan Railway, the world's first
underground line. **Theo Bergström**

Until the 1960s the emphasis in planning was on redevelopment rather than rehabilitation. Although the Smithfield area escaped substantial wartime damage, it has suffered from the same principles of large scale development applied elsewhere. Too often in the 1960s new buildings were designed with almost total disregard for their neighbours or their position in the street. True enough this is not peculiar to our time – the Georgians and Victorians often jostled new buildings uncompromisingly against the old. Our forefathers, however, tended to respect scale, if only because of their technical limitations. Today the sky is the limit.

The Barbican on the east side of Goswel Road is one of London's boldest and most massive post-war housing developments. The architecture is on a Roman scale, with colossal concrete pillars and spans dwarfing and ridiculing any human scale. The pedestrian, removed from ground level, is confined and easily disorientated. The oppressiveness and complexity of the Barbican contrasts extraordinarily with the simplicity and humanity of Smithfield's old streets and buildings. Chamberlin, Powell and Bon's Barbican scheme is a magnificent edifice of the post-war ideal, but no blueprint for the future.

Facing the Barbican along Goswell Road are several 1960s office blocks and a six-storey car park with rough mauve and grey concrete – decidedly brutalist. The *Daily Mirror* building at Holborn Circus is another crude 1960s glass and concrete slab, 170 feet high, with a windowless wall facing Holborn and vulgar scarlet-red glass. The new buildings on the north side of Holborn Viaduct are plain and dull, forming a weak apex at the corner with Charterhouse Street. Cardinal House on the corner of Cowcross Street and Farringdon Road is equally drab. Bart's Hospital has set a poor example with its post-war development, both in the medical school and in Bartholomew Close. Gloucester House nurses' home is far too high – a typically undistinguished utilitarian block. While the hospital must be encouraged to expand, a higher standard of design should be demanded.

There are some good new buildings; one of the best is the curved facade of the Golden Lane Estate fronting Goswell Road – an arcade of shops with flats above in a series of stepped projections, a modernistic Tudor style. Another is the new office building beside St. John's Gardens, a long low block with good quality brick forming a pleasant backcloth to the small public garden. Long Lane, Snow Hill, Turnmill Street and St. John's Lane all have some individually well designed new buildings, but too often they are set back from the old building line, usually because of planning requirements, or, like Priory House next to St. John's Gate, do not relate well to their neighbours. Dewhurst House in West Smithfield, completed in 1975, however, fits well into its surroundings despite its bulk and height, and contri-

Dewhurst's new building in St. John's
Lane, seen through the arch of St.
John's Gate.
Theo Bergström

butes greatly to the fine space of West Smithfield. Designed by Fitzroy Robinson, Dewhurst House has a high standard of materials and finishing with red brick and arched window lintels – a well conceived blend of traditional and modern.

HIGH BUILDINGS

Building height is extremely important in the setting of Smithfield's old buildings. The great majority of properties in Smithfield are between four and six storeys high. Gloucester House and Cardinal House are noticeable and regrettable exceptions. The Barbican towers, 412 feet high, are London's third highest structures, and loom over the area, disturbing the harmony of Cloth Fair and Charterhouse Square. It is vital that new buildings or extensions respect existing prevailing parapet and roof heights, so preserving the traditional character of Smithfield's streets. Even a badly-sited new lift-housing or water tank on an old building can ruin the skyline.

Limitations on Smithfield's building heights are also crucial to saving views of London's greatest landmark, the dome of St. Paul's cathedral. Height control regulations to protect views of St. Paul's were introduced in 1935, and have been imposed by the City Corporation for near views and by the G.L.C. for distant views. Both the controls and their application have been inadequate. Wren's dome has now all but disappeared among a forest of high blocks. Twenty years ago the city skyline seen from Primrose Hill or Parliament Hill was dominated by Wren's masterpiece; it was London's tallest building. Today the eye strains to make it out.

The lassitude in high building control shows where the true sympathies of the City authorities lie, and typifies the weakness of the G.L.C. in exerting real influence. Even the church authorities, who are entitled to veto the design of any building within half a mile of St. Paul's, have never raised any serious objection. One might even question the revered name of Sir William Holford who was responsible for the 1947 post-war plan for London and for the redevelopment of Paternoster Square, the precinct around St. Paul's. One of Holford's blocks almost completely obliterates the famous old view of St. Paul's from Farringdon Road. The new National Westminster Bank tower near Bishopsgate does not block any significant view but its sheer height, 600 feet, commands the sky, and will continue to do so until the next even higher tower. Roll on Manhattan.

Although most of the long Hampstead views of St. Paul's, and those from south of the Thames, have been ruined, there are still some impressive close views from the Smithfield area, at present unprotected. Two unforgettable views are from King Edward Street and from Aldersgate, where the full height of the dome and its supporting drum and pediment can be seen. Until 1974 the King Edward Street view was framed by Christchurch and pleasant Victorian buildings on the other side, all now demolished. The Post Office owns the huge island site south of Angel Street and cleared away the old buildings in 1974, intending to erect a gigantic new headquarters, whose height would block the views from Aldersgate and King Edward Street. Cuts in Post Office expenditure earned a reprieve, and gave the

One of today's few unspoilt views of St. Paul's framed by the 19th-century buildings of St. John Street; not a skyscraper in sight. **Theo Bergström**

archaeologists a tremendous chance for detailed examination of Roman and medieval remains on the site. Their excavations lasted six years and were well worth a visit before the bulldozers moved in.

One of the most remarkable views of St. Paul's dome is from St. John Street, north of its junction with Clerkenwell Road. The old Victorian commercial buildings of lower St. John Street provide a superb frame, with no modern high blocks in sight. This must be very rare now – the sort of view that was common in central London before the war. The greatest care is needed to preserve it. One extra storey or even a new lift-housing on the top of a building in Charterhouse Street or St. John Street could spoil or reduce the view.

Further north there are more distant views of the dome across Smithfield from the rising ground towards Islington, such as the Angel, Amwell Street, Percy Street and Myddelton Square. Often these are only fleeting glimpses through fortuitous gaps among buildings, but nonetheless they are part of the richness of the street scene, always a reminder to the Londoner or stranger of where he is.

Incredibly, only the vista from Farringdon Road is under statutory protection, and this is already ruined by Holford's monstrous block. Urgent action is required by Islington Council and the City Corporation to safeguard the other views by defining and enforcing maximum building heights along the lines of sight. Photomontages should be submitted with the plans for any proposed large or high building in the area.

THE WAY AHEAD

Smithfield is one of the nation's oldest urban areas and deserves a strong conservation policy. Some immediate environmental improvements could be fairly easily implemented. Apart from Charterhouse Square, St. John's Gardens, West Smithfield and Postman's Park, there are virtually no trees in the area. The barren pavements and huge buildings along Goswell Road and the dirt, noise and dilapidation along Farringdon Road could be mitigated by planting avenues of tall fastigiate forest trees.

Selective traffic management measures would improve several streets. The north end of Little Britain, for example, should be closed; it is used as a convenient short cut by Post Office vans whose speeds are a constant hazard to hospital staff. Traffic still thunders through St. John's Gate, at great risk to its structural safety.* While the road can be shut if Briset Street is widened, a few discreetly placed 'sleeping policemen' would deter through-traffic and reduce the speed and vibration of vehicles who service St. John's Lane. Charterhouse Street and Carthusian Street are also popular throughroutes which

*Thankfully, both St. John's Gate and Little Britain have now been closed to traffic.

disturb the peace of Charterhouse Square.

Despite the rich collection of ancient buildings, and its central position in London, Smithfield is not on the tourist trail. This may soon change. The new Museum of London at the corner of London Wall and Aldersgate has been an immense success. But at the moment thousands of visitors climb out of their coaches, tramp round the immaculate displays and cocooned exhibits and re-embark for the Tower or St. Paul's, oblivious of the wealth of history within a few minutes' walk. Perhaps the new museum at St. John's Gate, concerts in St. Bartholomew-the-Great and the new Barbican Arts Centre will bring more people to the area and put Smithfield on the map. Knick-knack shops and fancy boutiques are the last thing Smithfield needs, but evening and weekend opening for pubs and restaurants would be welcome. The City Corporation as part of European Architectural Heritage Year established two 'heritage walks' through the city, marked by direction discs in the pavement. One walk runs through part of the Smithfield area and could beneficially be extended north of the market to include St. John's Gate, Charterhouse and Clerkenwell: an ideal expedition for the kids.

The attitude to conservation has been sporadic. Planners have failed to resolve the conflicts between their different objectives. How long should vacant land or buildings be allowed to lie idle in the hope of obtaining the best land use on the site from an employment aspect? Should undesirable offices be refused in historic buildings where the fabric is decaying and industrial uses unlikely to be attracted? What aesthetic standards should be demanded for industrial buildings; are modern pre-fabricated units, cheap and efficient, acceptable in a conservation area? Should narrow medieval streets be widened so that large lorries can move more freely?

There is no simple yes/no answer to these questions – they depend on degree and circumstances. Different objectives must be balanced; over-emphasis on one will merely bring troubles elsewhere. The planner has an unenviable task. He carries the can for so much in the public eye and yet so many of the basic economic forces are completely beyond his control, like the decline of traditional industry or the escalation in construction costs. He even has little say about public expenditure. British Rail, for example, are proposing to electrify the St. Pancras line to Moorgate through the Farringdon Road cutting in 1982 and may also reopen the link to Holborn Viaduct (the tracks are currently used for storing the City Engineer's road salt and grit). London Transport are planning a new underground line for the 1980s from Chelsea to Hackney with a new station at Farringdon Road. What impact will such a public transport interchange have on the area? Surely it will focus yet more pressure for big office blocks?

The cry has gone up to save the inner city, but what are we trying to save? Is it jobs, or buildings, or particular activities? Should govern-

ment money be spent as at Pennybank Chambers, subsidising or promoting ventures that may in time turn out to be lame ducks? On the other hand, can the private developer be relied on to take risks which short term profit motives might not justify?

Smithfield has a unique character, with a rich and varied environment and a wealth of activities. The key to the area's future lies in this variety. Though some activities may die and be replaced by others, Smithfield has seen and accepted change before and can well do so again. A hundred years ago Smithfield was still an area where

Peters Lane 1880. A medieval street enclosed by medieval buildings.
Finsbury Library

people lived, worked, shopped, went to church, were educated, and amused themselves. Today this balance and diversity have suffered too much in favour of big business. If the full mosaic of human activity can be restored and enlivened, then Smithfield will regain its vitality. In this way, wider community interests will be protected and a cushion provided against dramatic change in the fortunes of any one activity. Conservation need not bring a stagnant and dying future, but diversity alone will keep Smithfield's history and tradition alive. Let us hope!

Peters Lane 1980. The old buildings are long gone. Now even the medieval street line is threatened by a Seifert office block. **Theo Bergström**

186 *Nos. 41-2 Cloth Fair, from the churchyard. Rare pre-Fire houses.*
Theo Bergström

TEN YEARS AFTER

As this book has shown, Smithfield is an area with buildings and institutions dating back to the Norman Conquest, and with a continuous history stretching over a thousand years. In this context, a decade may not seem very significant, but a comparison of the previous chapter with the current developments in Smithfield justifies a substantial review.

It is tempting to subscribe to the theory of accelerating change. Many people who know Smithfield would claim that the last ten years have brought change on an unprecedented scale, and fear that the next will bring even more. Perhaps this is too alarmist. Future generations may yet view the 1980s as a stable time, compared to the momentous upheavals of the 1530s when the medieval religious foundations were suppressed and plundered, or the 1860s when the fantastic engineering feats of constructing the railway and market were in progress. After all, the meat market is still here – just – together with Barts Hospital, The Charterhouse, St. John's Gate, many of the old buildings and the network of medieval streets. A degree of change is unavoidable, and indeed desirable, for no area can or should remain totally static either in fabric or activity. The real worry for those who love Smithfield is that pressures for change are mounting, like a dormant volcano. The 1980s enjoyed a climate which favoured conservation. A shift in the political or economic balance could herald the complete demise of Smithfield. The forces for change in the 1990s are ready and waiting; the leash is but a fine thread.

In 1980 the future of the meat market looked bleak. The throughput of meat had been declining steadily in the 1970s, while the authorities shrank from tackling long-term investment or planning. In 1982 Billingsgate fish market moved from its old site beside the Thames to Docklands. At the same time, positive plans emerged for

188 *Peters Lane, 1989, in the throes of
demolition and redevelopment.*
Theo Bergström

moving the Spitalfields vegetable market, also owned and run by the Corporation, to release its lucrative acres next to Broadgate. After years of ostrich-like indifference, attention at last turned to Smithfield. Decisions had to be taken, and quickly.

The Corporation set up a working party in 1984 to examine the future of the market and to explore all possible options. Five alternatives were considered: closure, relocation, major refurbishment, limited repairs, and 'do nothing'. The last two strategies were rightly eliminated as no more than costly procrastination. Closure and the abandonment of responsibility for running a meat market was ruled out, on the premise that London does need a wholesale market somewhere, and that the Corporation has a duty, by tradition and charter, to run it. Remember too, that Smithfield market has in the past, and could again, make a profit.

The relocation option was also rejected. The Billingsgate experience had burnt many fingers; removal costs escalated wildly above initial estimates; and Michael Heseltine's decision, as Secretary of State for the Environment, to list the old Victorian buildings in Lower Thames Street devalued the redevelopment potential. At Smithfield, Horace Jones' original market buildings are already listed, and in 1984 the GLC (since abolished) designated a Conservation Area to cover the rest. Protected views of St. Paul's from Farringdon Road and St. John Street would restrict the height of any new building, even if this was to be allowed.

Strategically Smithfield does not compare with Covent Garden or Spitalfields. The fruit and veg. trade is divided sectorally according to the supply routes and its dispersal to opposite sides of London, at Nine

Aldersgate Street, now almost entirely
redeveloped in the modern style; will
the same fate befall the rest of
Smithfield?
Theo Bergström

Elms and Temple Mills, makes geographic sense. Smithfield, however, is London's only meat market. Many tenants feared that relocation would cripple trade, particularly the central London hotel and catering custom. More worrying to the Corporation were the terms of the 1638 Royal Charter which stated that the land on which the market stands must return to Crown ownership should Smithfield cease to be used as a market! No doubt the Corporation would challenge the validity of these terms, but there could be no certainty of a waiver, and only the guarantee of a field day for the lawyers.

The Corporation wisely opted for major renovation and retention of the market. A modernized, compact market offered a realistic chance of survival and modest growth. The Central Markets Committee, advised by the City Architect and Market Superintendent, initially proposed retention of only the main market, disposing of the Poultry, General and Annexe markets and the cold stores in Charterhouse Street. The tenants protested vehemently that this would leave insufficient space, and would, effectively, finish off the market: the Poultry market, the most modern of all the buildings, should be kept, at least for the time being. This compromise was agreed by the Corporation in July 1987, allocating £14.3 million for refurbishing the main buildings and £¼ million for improving the Poultry market (April 1986 prices). Plans drawn up by the City Architect include a new layout of stalls to allow full access for fork-lift trucks, washable stainless steel floors and partitions, controlled temperature and humidity, cold storage and ancillary offices for traders in mezzanines, above and below, modern sanitation, and a new top floor of 91,000 square feet of general office space for let, serviced from the corner turrets. The scheme envisages four phases, tackling the work in quadrants, each taking nine months.

The package relies on major concessions from tenants and unions. Negotiations have proved tough, with deadlines set and extended, impasses confronted and bypassed. English Heritage have haggled over the internal alterations proposed to this historic and beautiful structure, balancing the welcomed repairs and improvements (such as removing the awful plastic canopies around the outside) with the loss of the majestic proportions and lofty airiness inside. The result has been delay and dramatically rising costs, to the point where the whole scheme is now in jeopardy.

New EEC proposals from Brussels seem likely to impose draconian food hygiene standards for the handling of meat and poultry which would not be met by the refurbishment scheme approved in 1987. Covered loading bay areas, with a controlled temperature of 5° centigrade, will now be required, to be implemented by 1st January, 1993. The idea of bringing large vehicles within the curtilage of the main market buildings had been considered at early feasibility stage and rejected, owing to the enormous problems and expense involved. Overall costs of a scheme to comply with the new regulations are now approaching three times those estimated in April 1986. The prospect of obtaining a viable return on such massive capital investment do not appear so bright. Despite a stabilization, even minor upturn, in the amount of meat handled by the market in the early 1980s, this has not been sustained, and trade has slackened alarmingly over the last year. The balance has undoubtedly shifted; the outlook appears pessimistic, and an announcement must be expected soon.

Meanwhile, no one knows the fate of the buildings west of the Poultry market; the Corporation, advised by the City Surveyor, seems reluctant to show its hand as to how these surplus buildings might be used or developed. The splendid Port of London cold store was listed in 1988, but badly gutted by fire in June 1989. Fortunately the façade survives, but the sooner these empty and neglected buildings find a saviour the better.

While debate and gossip over the market's future continues, the related meat trades have virtually vanished from the side streets. Cold stores, sausage-makers, smoke-houses, bacon-curers and offal merchants have all gone from Cowcross Street, St. John's Lane, Charterhouse Street and Bartholomew Close. Once familiar Smithfield names – Dumenil, Link, Legrand, Hedley Vicars and Rushbrook – are now memories, or a fading sign on a boarded shop-front. The predictions of ten years ago, ventured in the previous chapter, have become savagely true. Even the Smithfield Meat College in the former school in Eagle Court, which since 1947 has trained generations of apprentices, is now moving away from the

Dismantling the hotch-potch of
buildings in White Horse Alley
exposed these deserted smoke-houses.
Theo Bergström

immediate environs of the market. Some meat companies retain administrative offices in the area – Dewhurst's among the biggest, in new premises in St. John's Lane – showing traditional loyalty, but the local linkages are gone. The market is increasingly an island. A Smithfield address is no longer a prestigious necessity for the meat trade.

Despite this contraction Smithfield has not fallen into dereliction and decay – far from it. Most streets, both north and south of the market, have been a continuous building site as developers rush to redevelop and refurbish empty properties in a frenetic building boom. The vacation of so much floorspace has made Smithfield the prime candidate for speculators and property tycoons cashing in on the 'big-bang' expansion of the City of London. Improvements to the rail service through Farringdon, notably the electrified St. Pancras–Moorgate extension and the new Thameslink line, re-opening old tracks under Snowhill, have coincided with cheap land and low rents. Eager estate agents and promoters have conspiratorily trumpeted the historic charm and character of Smithfield and Clerkenwell, boosting the image of this segment of the City fringe.

Planning control previously exercised by Islington Council over the loss of industry and the spread of offices has been neutered by Central Government direction and new planning law. From 1987 planning permission was no longer required to change the use of a building from industry to offices. The floodgates were opened. Land and property values shot up, far outstripping rises elsewhere in London. Long-established local firms, fortunate enough to own their premises, were understandably tempted to cash in and move out.

Little Britain: an ominous web of scaffolding festoons the empty buildings around Postman's Park.
Theo Bergström

Many large firms have sold up and gone or are on their way – Booth's the gin distillers, Hammond and Champness, lift engineers, Swain's the printers, and Smith's who had been metal dealers in St. John's Square for two hundred years. Smaller businesses such as Gedges, Mitchell Inman and Albion Wire Works have gone too. The traditional industries rooted here since the Great Fire of London have evaporated within a decade. Jewellers and horologists who can make do with very small areas and who can afford the rents hang on, but for how much longer? Chapter Five already reads like an obituary.

Several familiar local landmarks have disappeared in recent years, including two old pubs – the Metropolitan on the corner of Clerkenwell and Farringdon Road, a faded gin palace allowed to grow shabby but retaining a faithful clientele until the final closing time; and the much lamented Magpie and Stump opposite the Old Bailey, from whose upper floors prurient voyeurs had cheered the executions at Newgate gaol. No prizes for guessing what replaces them. The derelict hulk of the Farringdon Goods depot, bombed, empty and unrepaired since the war, was finally demolished in 1989. Despite a feasible scheme for refurbishment and its historic interest as the original terminus of the world's first underground line, the Department of the Environment rejected requests for preservation. 'A new City landmark' is how the agents extol Seifert's Farringdon Court which rises on the site: scarcely a 'court', more a wall of glass and granite to turn Farringdon Road into a canyon. The occupiers will dislike the scruffy book market outside which somehow struggles on against all odds. Mr. Jeffery, still operating from his ramshackle store in Clerkenwell Close, refuses to move to the improved Exmouth Market up the road and defiantly stands his ground with his loyal punters, hemmed in by traffic and scaffolding. When he quits, Islington Council will discontinue the pitches and another fragment of London life will become history.

Great controversy has surrounded the Danish Bacon site, a large chunk of land between Cowcross Street, Peters Lane, St. John's Lane and Britton Street. A long campaign by Land and Property Trust PLC to buy out owners and tenants resulted in a planning application to redevelop, keeping just a few of the buildings in Cowcross Street. This comprehensive scheme will change the character of the area, with two large office blocks replacing the higgledy-piggledy assemblage of old buildings in White Horse Alley and opening up the northern end of Peters Lane. Demolition began soon after planning consent was granted; the late eighteenth-century tenements in St. John's Lane were among the first to go, and then the smoke-houses behind, bulldozers ripping open their blackened insides for a last fleeting glimpse.

The archaeologists were given a few hectic weeks to explore, working quickly and skilfully to expose unsuspected remains.

Beneath No. 1 St. John's Lane, ironically the oldest building pulled down, the clunch-and-ragstone footings of a medieval gatehouse were unearthed, straddling the bottom of St. John's Lane. This suggests that the original precinct of St. John's Priory was larger than previously thought and extended south down to Cowcross Street, and perhaps as far west as the banks of the River Fleet along Turnmill Street. After the sacking by Wat Tyler in 1381, which probably destroyed the gatehouse and many other buildings, the Priory very likely contracted: Docwra's new gateway, still standing, was built further north enclosing a smaller precinct. Pieces of carved stone window tracery and German millstone and several decorated glazed floor-tiles, one bearing the arms of the prior from about 1380, were found among the honeycomb foundations of cellars and outbuildings, hidden for centuries beneath Tudor, Georgian and Victorian buildings. The stunning revelation of this medieval substrata was short-lived; within days the pile-drivers and diggers had moved in, destroying these ancient relics for ever.

The Museum of London's archaeologists have also had a bonanza on the north side of St. John's Square, immediately next to the Priory Church. Here a co-operative developer has generously allowed adequate time for the discovery of part of the fourteenth-century nave wall which replaced the original round church. Beside the wall, graves of children and pregnant women were uncovered, presumably the remains of unfortunate foundlings and destitutes taken in by the Priory. Beneath Nos. 47 and 48 St. John's Square, superb Tudor brick vaults, spanning medieval stone foundations, have been revealed;

194

*Archaeologists sifting through the
medieval strata at St. John's Lane,
Summer 1989.*
Theo Bergström

hopefully they will be preserved as a new subterranean wine bar under the Georgian buildings above.

Less happily, the Little Britain project blunders on, inexorably and execrably. Behind the propped tombstone façades of the old buildings a steel-and-concrete monster begins to emerge which will change the skyline south of the market. When the road is completed linking Newgate Street with London Wall, the last foolish piece of the 1960s jigsaw will be slotted into place. Farewell, Cox's Court and Cross Keys Square. The City Corporation's bullish paranoia about the rival threat of Canary Wharf as London's new financial centre has promoted Terry Farrell's gigantic monstrosity which now dwarfs the dual carriageway. For all their drawbacks, the walkways of London Wall projected a sense of space and openness when originally conceived, which was much appreciated by Pevsner. Now even that is fast disappearing; claustrophobes keep clear!

The 1980s have, nevertheless, seen some welcome new building and good design. The award-winning Charterhouse Mews peeps invitingly over the Charterhouse boundary wall. The gabled mellow brick of Dewhurst's new offices on the corner of St. John's Lane and Briset Street has the right scale to draw the eye to St. John's Gate, complementing but not competing. The bombed gaps in Long Lane are now filled unostentatiously. New houses and the richly decorated livery halls of the Founders and the Farmers and Fletchers in Cloth Fair and Middle Street have captured and enhanced the charm of these narrow lanes. After much fuss, Janet Street Porter's house in Britton Street, by Piers Gough, is becoming accepted, even liked by some. Cleverly graded bricks and a bright blue roof suggest a

The White Horse Inn, Little Britain,
just its façade propped as a punctured
screen against the massive new
buildings behind.
Theo Bergström

WIMPEY
Breaking new ground

WIMPEY
Breaking new ground.

WIMPEY   WIMPEY

restrained Gaudi, perhaps. It has certainly earned Ms. Porter immortality locally, even if she no longer chooses to live there.

An element of quirkiness is far preferable to the disappointingly
bland edifice by the same architects at the bottom of St. John Street,
sadly not the only example of uninspired post-modernism in the
locality. Most of the new blocks fronting Aldersgate Street are flatly
dull, garnished with stick-on gimmicks. Good modern design stands

*Sadly, many old buildings and
ancient ground were broken to realize
Wimpey's brave slogan.*
Theo Bergström

the test of time; YRM's convincing building overlooking the Benjamin Street gardens has now been added into the conservation area. Sensitive and simple refurbishments, such as Nos. 14–16 Cowcross Street and the former distillery depot on the corner of Turnmill Street and Clerkenwell Road, are admirable, but elsewhere roof extensions, chiller tanks and lift machinery, supposedly out of sight, all too often end up being eyesores on old buildings.

The Prince of Wales' 'Vision of Britain' has focused widespread attention on design and generated heated debate. His courageous unpretentious intervention may yet ensure that Sudbury House, the worst of Holford's Paternoster Square disasters, is demolished and replaced by lower buildings, thus reinstating the long-lost view of St. Paul's dome from Farringdon Road. Cardinal House, an equally ugly block on the corner of Cowcross Street may go too if the East-West Cross Rail proposal is approved, linking Paddington and Liverpool Street with a new station beneath Smithfield. Perhaps our vision of Smithfield can be refreshed over the next decade by these and other improvements.

Barts Hospital continues to expand and modernize on its ancient site. The new children's unit facing West Smithfield and Little Britain is the most visible extension, sympathetically designed to blend with the old stone buildings. The immediate prospect of relocating the medical college has receded. New student accommodation and laboratories are under construction on the empty sites in Goswell and Clerkenwell Roads.

Without doubt, Smithfield and Clerkenwell have become increasingly popular with visitors from far and near. The Heritage

The most talked-about architecture in
Smithfield – Janet Street Porter's
house in Britton Street.
Theo Bergström

Centre in St. John's Square has developed as an enthusiastic hub for tourism, promoting Clerkenwell as London's 'hidden village'. There are specialist visitors – researchers seeking ancestral lineage from the Society of Genealogists in Charterhouse Buildings, horological historians, and architectural students galore – but there is potential for far more. The museum in St. John's Gate is attractively run, but the Charterhouse remains a private secret gem and the Marx Mem-

Founders' Hall, Cloth Fair, much acclaimed, and recalling the terrace demolished in 1905 (see page 75).
Theo Bergström

orial Library in Clerkenwell Green could be better geared to visitors. Many pubs and the proliferation of restaurants are now crowded with affluent City and West End folk – Rudland and Stubbs in Cowcross Street, the Crown in Clerkenwell Green, the City Pride in Farringdon Lane, and the Fox and Anchor in Charterhouse Street – and busy in the evenings, unheard of ten years ago. Smithfield is fashionable, a place to go and be seen. Gentrification was a word of the 1970s in the up-and-coming parts of London; yuppification is the 1980s catchphrase, and much apparent in Smithfield.

The Smithfield Trust has proved a much needed and heeded local voice in the area, constantly campaigning and ever vigilant, but deserving of wider support and membership. As feared in the previous chapter, the Smithfield Area Plan, approved in the late 1970s, proved to be limited in its guidance and inspiration, weak in its precision and prescription. After a decade of indecision and frustration, both Islington Council and the City Corporation in 1989 adopted more rigorous planning policies to counterbalance the increasing threat to the historic character of Smithfield. As part of a series of conservation guidelines, Islington has identified all the buildings in their patch where they would not allow demolition, under any circumstances. When few buildings are statutorily listed, the replacement of all the others with modern buildings, even if well designed, would not result in the preservation or enhancement of the Conservation Area. The fabric of Smithfield has evolved over a thousand years; structures survive from nine different centuries.

In 1989 this superb fragment of the medieval Charterhouse cloister wall was uncovered beneath the tennis courts near Goswell Road.
Theo Bergström

199

This incremental diversity must be retained. There is still room for
some good new building, particularly to replace the worst horrors of
the 1950s and 60s, so long as it blends and harmonises with its
neighbours, respecting established building lines and street pattern.
Controls to limit heights to five storeys and horizontal scale to
prevent 'ground-scrapers' are essential. Comprehensive developments, sweeping away ancient alleys and courts and replacing a
dozen old buildings with one monolithic hulk must be fiercely
opposed. The sensitive adaptation of old properties to meet modern
requirements must be fostered instead. Ten years ago dereliction and
disinterest was a problem; now there is too much interest, too much
investment, and a real danger that the character of Smithfield, so
vaunted by the developers, will be destroyed by their own excesses.

Fabric alone, however, does not determine the feel of an area.
Variety of activity is equally crucial to Smithfield. The planning
authorities' proposal to insist on mixed uses within all new development, to encourage residential, shops, showrooms, community workshops, eating- and drinking-places, are excellent. They must be
allowed to succeed in order to offset the seemingly unending tide of
monotonous office building. Failure of these policies will result in a
plush uniformity of sterile offices with a smattering of expensive
restaurants, and a sprinkling of 'heritage' buildings set in an ocean of
speculative mediocrity.

Smithfield remains London's oldest and most special faubourg. If it
is to survive it must do so as a community, with all the richness and
intricate dependency which this demands. The complex tapestry of
buildings and activities must be maintained and enhanced. Every-

200 *Expensive restaurants now abound in
Smithfield, this one in Sir John's
beloved Cloth Fair.*
Theo Bergström

body involved with Smithfield, whether as a resident, worker, land-owner, developer, architect, planner or politician, has a duty to make sure that this happens, before it is too late.

This sketch review of the 1980s begs more questions than it answers. What lies ahead for Smithfield in the next ten years? Will Smithfield market survive the coming decade? Will the Channel Tunnel with its proposed terminus station at Kings Cross and the

Charterhouse Mews, tucked away
behind the Charterhouse wall,
meticulously detailed, and a model for
others to follow.
Theo Bergström

East-West Cross Rail fuel ever more pressure for change, or will the rampant building boom subside and bypass Smithfield? How will we look back in A.D. 2000, with nostalgia or pride? It is an intriguing prospect.

This warehouse in Greenhill Rents has been readily converted to provide splendid studio and office space.
Theo Bergström

BIBLIOGRAPHY

Betjeman, J. *Victorian and Edwardian London*, Batsford 1969

Boswell, J. *The Life of Samuel Johnson* 1st edn. 1791

Central London Planning Conference *Draft Advisory Plan for Central London* 1976

Corporation of London *Smithfield District Plan 1978*

Dickens, C. *Great Expectations* 1860

Dickens, C. *Oliver Twist* 1838

Dodd, C. *Food in London* 1858

Finsbury Old People's Welfare Committee *Memories of Finsbury 1880–1900 by old residents* 1955

Greater London Council *London: the future and your employment* 1973

Greater London Council *Greater London Development Plan* 1976

Gripaios, P. *Industrial decline in London: an examination of its causes* Urban Studies 1977

Islington, London Borough of *Smithfield Area Plan* 1978

Jenkins, S. *A city at risk* Hutchinson 1970

Keeble, D. E. *Industrial decentralisation and the metropolis* Transactions of the Institute of British Geographers 1968

Knowles, D. and Grimes, W. F. *Charterhouse. The Medieval Foundation in the light of recent discoveries* Longmans 1954

King, E. and Luke H. *The Knights of St. John in the British realm* Hills and Lacy 1967

Lehmann, J. *Holborn* Macmillan 1970

Lloyd, D. (ed.) *Save the City* Society for the Protection of Ancient Buildings/Civic Trust/Georgian Group/Victorian Society 1976

Marshall, D. *Dr. Johnson's London* Wiley and Sons 1968

Mayhew, H. *London Labour and the London Poor* 1851

Medvei and Thornton (ed.) *The Royal Hospital of Saint Bartholomew 1123–1973* St. Bartholomew's Hospital 1974

Mee, A. *The King's England; London north of the Thames* Hodder and Stoughton 1972

Mee, A. *The King's England; London City and Westminster* Hodder and Stoughton 1975

Moore, N. *The history of St. Bartholomew's Hospital* (2 vols) Pearson 1918

Morley, H. *Memoirs of Bartholomew Fair* Frederick Warne and Co. 1890

National Board for Prices and Incomes *Report No. 126: Smithfield Market* HMSO 1969

Pevsner, N. (revised by B. Cherry) *The Buildings of England; London, the cities of London and Westminster* 3rd edn. Penguin 1973

Robertson, D. W. *Chaucer's London* Wiley and Sons 1968

Rudé, G. *Hanoverian London 1714–1808* Secker and Warburg 1971

Schwab I. *The archaeology of Islington* Inner London Archaeological Unit 1978

Sheppard, F. *London 1808–1870: the infernal wen* Secker and Warburg 1971

Stow, J. *The survey of London* 1st. edn. 1598

Trevelyan, G. M. *English social history* Longmans 1942

Webb, E. A. *The records of St. Bartholomew's Smithfield* (2 vols.) Oxford University Press 1921

Williams, G. G. *Guide to Literary London* Batsford 1973

Wilson, A. *London's industrial heritage* David and Charles 1967

Zwart, P. *Islington: a history and guide* Sidgwick and Jackson 1973

204   *Cloth Fair in 1912, a corner shop serving local people, both long gone. Note Mitchell Inman and the Rising Sun in the distance.* **G.L.C.**

205